New Jersey
NOTARY
PRIMER

The NNA's Handbook
for New Jersey Notaries

Thirteenth Edition

Published by

National Notary Association
9350 De Soto Avenue
Chatsworth, CA 91311-4926
Telephone: (800) 876-6827
Fax: (818) 700-0920
Website: NationalNotary.org
Email: nna@NationalNotary.org

The information in this *Primer* is correct and current at the
time of its publication, although new laws, regulations and
rulings may subsequently affect the validity of certain sections.
This information is provided to aid comprehension of state
Notary Public requirements and should not be construed as
legal advice. Please consult an attorney for inquiries relating to
legal matters.

Thirteenth Edition ©2023
First Edition ©1994

ISBN: 978-1-59767-315-0

Table of Contents

Have a Tough Notary Question?

If you were a National Notary Association member, you could get the answer to that difficult question. Join the NNA° and your membership includes access to the NNA° Hotline* and live Notary experts providing the latest Notary information regarding laws, rules and regulations.

Hours

Monday – Friday	5:00 a.m.–6:30 p.m. (PT)
Saturday	5:00 a.m.–5:00 p.m. (PT)

NNA° Hotline Toll-Free Phone Number: 1-888-876-0827

After hours you can leave a message or email our experts at Hotline@NationalNotary.org and they will respond the next business day.

*Access to the NNA° Hotline is for National Notary Association members and NNA° Hotline subscribers only. Call and become a member today.

Introduction

You are to be commended on your interest in New Jersey Notary law! Purchasing the *New Jersey Notary Primer* identifies you as a conscientious professional who takes your official responsibilities seriously.

In few fields is the expression "more to it than meets the eye" truer than in Notary law. What often appears on the surface to be a simple procedure may, in fact, have important legal considerations.

The purpose of the *New Jersey Notary Primer* is to provide you with a resource to help decipher the many intricate laws that affect notarization. In doing so, the *Primer* will acquaint you with all important aspects of New Jersey's Notary law and with prudent Notary practices in general.

The *New Jersey Notary Primer* takes you through the myriad of Notary laws and puts them in easy-to-understand terms. Every section of the law is analyzed and explained, as well as topics not covered by New Jersey law but nonetheless of vital concern to you as a Notary.

Whether you're about to be commissioned for the first time, or are a longtime Notary, we're sure the *New Jersey Notary Primer* will provide you with new insight and understanding. Your improved comprehension of New Jersey's Notary law will naturally result in your greater competence as a professional Notary Public.

Milton G. Valera
Chairman
National Notary Association

The Notary Appointment

Additional information about New Jersey's requirements for Notaries Public is available on the Department of the Treasury's website. For step-by-step instructions on the commission application process, applicants also may visit NationalNotary.org.

THE NOTARY COMMISSION

Application for New Commission

Qualifications. To become a Notary in New Jersey, whether as a first-time Notary or to renew a commission, the applicant (NJSA 52:7-12; 52:7-13; 52:7-20 and 52:7-21):

- Must be at least 18 years old.

- Must be a resident of New Jersey or a resident of an adjoining state who maintains or has a place of employment or practice in New Jersey.

- Must not have been convicted in New Jersey or another state of an offense involving dishonesty or of a crime in the first or second degree.

Denial of Application. No one may be appointed or reappointed as a New Jersey Notary who has been convicted of a crime of the second degree or above, of an offense involving dishonesty (e.g., forgery, counterfeiting) under the laws of New Jersey, or of a substantially similar crime under the laws of another state or of the United States (NJSA 52:7-20, 52:7-21).

Application Fee. The application and $25 application fee must be submitted electronically to the State Treasurer (NJSA 52:7-11). An additional fee will be required at the time of filing the Notary Public's certificate of commission and qualification with the county clerk (NJSA 22A:2-29).

Application for Reappointment

Application. A Notary seeking reappointment must apply for a new commission and follow the same procedures as when applying for a commission for the first time (NJSA 52:7-11).

Education and Exam

Course. Required for initial and renewal Notary applicants. Non-attorney applicants for an initial Notary commission and renewal applicants for a commission who have previously completed the educational requirements or were commissioned before October 20, 2022, must comply with state educational and testing requirements (NJSA 52:7-10.10.2.b and c).

Exam. Required for initial Notary applicants (NJSA 52:7-10.3).

Notary Bond and Liability

Not Required. New Jersey Notaries are not required to obtain a surety bond.

Liability. As ministerial officials, Notaries generally may be held financially responsible for any and all damages caused by their mistakes or misconduct in performing notarial acts.

If a person is financially injured by a Notary's negligence or failure to properly execute a notarial act — whether performed intentionally or unintentionally — the Notary may be sued in civil court and ordered to pay all resulting damages, including attorneys' fees.

A person need not be named in a document in order to sue a Notary for damages resulting from the Notary's handling of that document. If, for example, a lender accepts a forged, notarized deed as collateral for a loan, the lender might sue to recover losses from the Notary who witnessed the notarized deed.

Errors and Omissions Insurance. Notaries may choose to purchase insurance to cover any unintentional errors or omissions they may make. Notary errors and omissions insurance provides protection for Notaries who are involved in claims or sued for damages resulting from unintentional notarial errors and omissions. In the event of a claim or civil lawsuit, the insurance company will provide and pay for the Notary's legal counsel and absorb any damages levied by a court or agreed to in a settlement, up to the policy coverage limit. Errors and omissions insurance does not cover the Notary for dishonest, fraudulent or criminal acts or omissions, or for willful or intentional disregard of the law.

Oath of Office

Requirement. New Jersey Notaries are required to take and file an oath of office before executing any acts as a Notary Public (NJSA 52:7-14).

Filing the Oath. The oath must be taken and filed with the clerk of the county in which the Notary resides within three months of the commission start date indicated on the Notary's certificate of commission and qualification. Nonresident applicants must take the oath before the clerk of the county in New Jersey in which the applicant maintains an office or is employed.

To take the oath, the applicant must bring the Notary's certificate of commission and qualification to the clerk of the county in which he or she resides or is employed. The clerk will then administers the required oath, in which the applicant swears to faithfully and honestly discharge the duties of the office of Notary Public for New Jersey.

Within 10 days after administering the oath, the county clerk returns the certificate of commission and qualification to the State Treasurer and records the "sworn date" in the county clerk's files (NJSA 52:7-14).

A Notary may choose to file additional copies of the certificate of commission and qualification in other counties. Although the Notary has statewide jurisdiction, filing additional certificates makes it easier for a county clerk to authenticate a Notary's commission if the Notary lives and works in different counties. However, filing duplicate certificates is not required (NJSA 52:7-15).

Fee. The county clerk will charge a fee to administer the oath and another fee to file and record it (NJSA 22A:2-29). The Notary applicant should contact the local county clerk to determine these fees.

Failure to File Oath of Office. A Notary Public must file his or her oath of office within three months after the date specified on the Notary Public's commission certificate. Failure to file within this time limit may result in cancellation or revocation of the appointment (NJSA 52:7-14).

Jurisdiction

Statewide. Resident and nonresident (working in New Jersey) New Jersey Notaries may perform official acts throughout the state, but not beyond the state borders (NJSA 52:7-15).

A Notary may not witness a signing outside of New Jersey and then return to the state to perform the notarization. All parts of a given notarization must be performed at the same time and place within the state of New Jersey.

Term of Office

Five-Year Term. The term of office for a New Jersey Notary Public is five years. Each term begins on the date specified by the State Treasurer on the commission certificate and ends at midnight on its commission expiration date or as deemed necessary by the State Treasurer (NJSA 52:7-11).

Resignation

Notification. To resign, a Notary should submit a written notice to the State Treasurer, giving an effective date. Such a resignation is appropriate if the Notary moves and does not retain a place of business or office in New Jersey. It is recommended the notice be sent by certified mail.

The resignation notice may also be sent to the office of the clerk of the county where the Notary has filed the certificate of commission and qualification.

Disposition of Seal and Records. When a Notary resigns, the required stamp should be destroyed or defaced to prevent fraudulent use.

In regards to the journal of notarial acts, the Notary must either:

1. retain the journal for 10 years after the performance of the last notarial act chronicled in the journal; or

2. transmit the journal to the Department of the Treasury, Division of Revenue and Enterprise Services, or a repository approved by the State Treasurer.

Death of Notary

Notification. If a Notary dies, the Notary's personal representative should notify the State Treasurer. The notification should include the Notary's name and commission number, as well as any additional pertinent information, and should be sent by certified mail.

Disposition of Seal and Records. On the death or adjudication of incompetency of a current or former Notary, the Notary's personal representative or guardian or any other person knowingly in possession of the journal shall, within 45 days, transmit it to the Department of the Treasury, Division of Revenue and Enterprise Services, or a repository approved by the State Treasurer. The Notary's stamp should be destroyed.

Change of Address

Notification Required. When a Notary changes his or her address, notification must be made to the State Treasurer — and to all county clerks where copies of the certificate of commission and qualification are filed — before notarizing any documents.

Change of address forms are available at www.state.nj.us/treasury/revenue/notarychange.pdf or by calling (609) 292-9292.

The Notary must return the change of address form and a $25 fee (payable to the State Treasurer) by certified mail to:

> State of New Jersey
> Department of the Treasury
> Division of Revenue and Enterprise Services
> Notary Public Section
> P.O. Box 452 Trenton, NJ 08646

Change of Name

Notification Required. When a Notary changes his or her name, notification must be made to the State Treasurer before notarizing any documents (NJSA 52:7-18).

Change of name forms are available at www.state.nj.us/treasury/revenue/notarychange.pdf or by calling (609) 292-9292.

The Notary must return the change of name form and a $25 fee (payable to the State Treasurer) by certified mail to the Notary Public Section at the address above. Once a name change form has been filed, the Notary must notarize using the new name (NJSA 52:7-18).

Commission Certificate. A New Jersey Notary who files a change of name form with the State Treasurer also may request a new commission certificate indicating the new name, though this is not required.

The request should be made when filing the name change form and must be accompanied by a $1 fee, in addition to the $25 fee for filing the name change. ▦

Screening the Signer

Personal Appearance

Required. New Jersey law expressly requires document signers to personally appear before the Notary at the time of notarization (NJSA 46:14-2.1). For traditional and in-person electronic notarizations, this means that the Notary and the signer must both be physically present, face to face in the same room, when the notarization takes place. For remote notarizations, the Notary and signer must meet face-to-face using live, audio-video communication technology. Notarizations may never be performed over the telephone.

Willingness

Confirmation. New Jersey Notaries are required to confirm that the signer is signing willingly (*New Jersey Notary Public Manual*).

To confirm willingness, the Notary need only ask the document signers if they are signing of their own free will. If a signer does or says anything that makes the Notary think the signer is being pressured to sign, the Notary must refuse to notarize.

Awareness

Confirmation. New Jersey Notaries are required to confirm that the signer is aware of what he or she is signing (*New Jersey Notary Public Manual*).

To confirm awareness, the Notary simply makes a layperson's judgment about the signer's ability to understand what he or she is signing. A document signer who cannot respond intelligibly in a simple conversation with the Notary should not be considered sufficiently aware to sign at that moment. If the notarization is taking place in a medical environment, the signer's doctor can be consulted for a professional opinion. Otherwise, if the signer's awareness is in doubt, the Notary must refuse to notarize.

Foreign-Speaking Signers. There should always be direct communication between the Notary and document signer — whether in English or any other language. The Notary should never rely on an intermediary or interpreter to determine a signer's willingness or awareness. A third party may have a motive for misrepresenting the circumstances to the Notary and/or to the signer.

Identifying Document Signers

Required. In notarizing a signature on any document, New Jersey Notaries are required by law to identify the signer (NJSA 46:14-2.1). The *New Jersey Notary Public Manual* stipulates that Notaries must identify all signers, regardless of the type of notarial act.

Three Identification Methods. The following three methods of identification are acceptable:

- The Notary's personal knowledge of the signer's identity (see "Personal Knowledge of Identity," below)

- The oath or affirmation of a credible identifying witness (see "Credible Identifying Witnesses," pages 10–11)

- Reliable identification documents or ID cards (see "Identification Documents," pages 11–13)

Personal Knowledge of Identity

Definition. The safest and most reliable method of identifying a document signer is for the Notary to depend on his or her own personal knowledge of the signer's identity. Personal knowledge means familiarity with an individual resulting from interactions with that person over a period of time sufficient to eliminate any reasonable doubt that the person has the identity claimed. The familiarity should come from association with the individual in relation to other people and should be based upon a chain of circumstances surrounding the individual.

New Jersey law does not specify how long a Notary must be acquainted with an individual before personal knowledge of identity may be claimed. The Notary's common sense must prevail. In general, the longer the Notary is acquainted with a person, and the more interactions the Notary has had with that person, the more likely the individual is indeed personally known.

For instance, the Notary might safely regard a friend since childhood as personally known, but the Notary would be foolish to consider a person met for the first time the previous day as such. Whenever the Notary has a reasonable doubt about a signer's identity, that individual should be considered not personally known, and the identification should be made through other acceptable methods: either a credible identifying witness or reliable identification documents.

Credible Identifying Witnesses

Purpose. When a document signer is not personally known to the Notary and is not able to present reliable ID cards, that signer may be identified on the oath or affirmation of a credible identifying witness. This procedure is considered to provide "satisfactory evidence" of the signer's identity.

Qualifications. Every credible identifying witness must personally know the document signer. The credible identifying witness also must be personally known by the Notary or must present an acceptable ID card. In a sense, a credible identifying witness is a walking, talking ID card.

A credible identifying witness should have a reputation for honesty. The witness should be a competent, independent individual who won't be tricked, bullied, or otherwise influenced into identifying someone he or she does not really know. In addition, the witness should have no direct personal interest in the transaction requiring a notarial act.

Oath (Affirmation) for Credible Identifying Witness. The Notary must administer an oath or affirmation to the credible identifying witness in order to compel truthfulness.

If not otherwise prescribed by law, the following or similar wording may be used by a New Jersey Notary:

> Do you solemnly swear that you know the signer truly is the person he/she claims to be, so help you God?
>
> (Do you solemnly affirm that you know the signer truly is the person he/she claims to be?)

Journal Entry. Each credible identifying witness must sign the Notary's journal in the place where the Notary indicates the method of identification of the signer. The Notary must also print each witness's name and address. If the credible witness is identified with an ID card, the Notary must provide the ID information of the witness in the journal.

Not a Subscribing Witness. Notaries must not confuse a credible identifying witness with a subscribing witness. A credible identifying witness vouches for the identity of a signer who appears before the Notary. A subscribing witness vouches for the genuineness of the signature of a person who does not appear before the Notary. (See "Proof of Execution by Subscribing Witness," pages 36–38.)

Identification Documents (ID Cards)

Acceptable Identification Documents. Notaries are allowed to use reliable identification documents (ID cards) to identify document signers whom they do not personally know. Such cards are considered to be "satisfactory evidence" of the signer's identity.

New Jersey law specifies that these identification documents are sufficient if they are current or expired not more than three years before the performance of the notarial act:

- a passport

- driver's license

- government-issued, non-driver identification card

- or another form of government-issued identification, which contains the individual's signature or a photograph of the individual's face; and is satisfactory to the notarial officer.

Multiple Identification. While one good identification document or card may be sufficient to identify a signer, the Notary may always ask for more, especially if the Notary has reasons to suspect that the signer has presented fraudulent identification.

Unacceptable Identification Documents. Because they are easily counterfeited, Social Security cards, birth certificates, and credit cards are worthless as primary identifying documents.

Name Variations. The Notary must make sure that the name on the document is the same as the name appearing on the identification presented.

In certain circumstances, it may be acceptable for the name on the document to be an abbreviated form of the name on the ID; for example, John D. Smith instead of John David Smith. Last names or surnames, however, should always be the same.

Fraudulent Identification. Identification documents are the least secure of the three methods of identifying a document signer, because phony ID cards are common. The Notary should scrutinize each card for evidence of tampering or counterfeiting, or for evidence that it is a genuine card that has been issued to an impostor.

Some clues that an ID card may have been fraudulently altered include mismatched type styles, a photograph with a raised surface, a signature that does not match the signature on the document, unauthorized lamination of the card, and smudges, erasures, smears and discolorations.

Possible tip-offs to a counterfeit ID card include misspelled words, a brand new-looking card with an old date of issuance, two cards with exactly the same photograph showing the bearer in identical clothing or with an identical background, and inappropriate patterns and features.

Indications that an identification card may have been issued to an impostor include the birthdate or address on the card being unfamiliar to the bearer and all the ID cards seeming brand new.

Signature by Mark

Mark Serves as Signature. A person who cannot sign his or her name because of illiteracy or a physical disability may instead use a mark — an "X", for example — as a signature (NJSA 46:14-4.2).

Witnesses. For a signature by mark to be notarized, the National Notary Association recommends that there be two witnesses to the making of the mark in addition to the Notary.

Both witnesses should sign the document and the Notary's journal. One witness should legibly print the marker's name beside the mark on the document. It is recommended that a mark also be affixed in the Notary's journal.

Notarization Procedures. Because a properly witnessed mark is considered a signature under custom and law, no special Notary certificate is required. As required with any other signer, the marker must be positively identified.

Signature by Proxy

Designated Individual. If an individual is physically unable to sign a record, the individual may direct another person other than the notarial officer to sign the record with the individual's name.

Required Notation. In notarizing a record for an individual physically unable to sign, the Notary must insert "Signature affixed by (name of other individual) at the direction of (name of individual)" or words of similar import (NJSA 52:7-10.11).

Notarizing for Minors

Persons Under Age 18. Generally, individuals must reach the age of majority before they can handle their own legal affairs and sign documents for themselves. In New Jersey, the age of majority is 18. Normally, parents or court-appointed guardians will sign on a minor's behalf. In certain cases, where minors are engaged in business transactions or serving as witnesses in court, they may lawfully sign documents and have their signatures notarized.

Include Age Next to Signature. When notarizing for a minor, the Notary should ask the young signer to write his or her age next to the signature to alert any person relying on the document that the signer is a minor. The Notary is not required to verify the minor signer's age.

Identification. The method for identifying a minor is the same as that for an adult. However, determining the identity of a minor can be a problem, because minors often do not possess acceptable identification documents such as driver's licenses or passports. If the minor does not have an acceptable ID, then the other methods of identifying signers must be used, either the Notary's personal knowledge of the minor or the oath or affirmation of a credible identifying witness who can identify the minor. (See "Credible Identifying Witnesses," pages 10–11.)

Refusal of Services

Noncustomers. An employer may limit the services of Notary employees to business-related notarizations during hours of employment and exclude services to the general public. Notary-employees may refuse to notarize for noncustomers if their employer has limited their services in this manner.

Discrimination. Notaries should honor all lawful and reasonable requests to notarize. A person's race, age, gender, religion, nationality, ethnicity, lifestyle or political viewpoint is never legitimate cause for refusing to perform a notarial act.

Penalty. Should a Notary refuse to perform a lawfully requested notarial act — other than when restricted by the Notary's employer as described above — the Notary may be subject to charges of discrimination and liable to the injured party for any damages.

Exception. A Notary may refuse to notarize a document if the officer is not satisfied that:

a. the individual executing the record is competent or has the capacity to execute the record;

b. the individual's signature is knowingly and voluntarily made;

c. the individual's signature on the record or statement substantially conforms to the signature on a form of identification used to determine the identity of the individual; or

d. the physical appearance of the individual signing the record or statement substantially conforms to the photograph on a form of identification used to determine the identity of the individual.

Employer/Notary Agreement

Agreement to Limit Notary's Services. A Notary Public employed by a financial institution may agree to follow the employer's direction or policy to not administer oaths except in the course of business. The restriction is limited to the Notary's service during regular business hours and is valid only if the Notary agrees to the policy. In this context, a "financial institution" is specifically defined as a state or federally chartered bank, savings bank, savings and loan association, or credit union (NJSA 41:2-3).

It may be helpful to the Notary to have the agreement in writing to prevent any haggling when limiting these services. If the Notary is challenged, the written agreement may serve as evidence that this is the employer's consistent policy, perhaps protecting the Notary and the employer from charges of discrimination. ■

Reviewing the Document

Blank or Incomplete Documents

Do Not Notarize. While New Jersey law does not specifically address notarizing a blank or incomplete document, the National Notary Association strongly advises against this practice.

Any blanks in a document should be filled in by the signer prior to notarization. If the blanks are inapplicable and intended to be left unfilled, the signer should line through each space or write "Not Applicable" or "N/A." The Notary may not, however, tell the signer what to write in the blanks. If the signer is unsure how to fill in the blanks, he or she should contact the document's issuer, its eventual recipient, or an attorney.

Photocopies & Faxes

Original Signature. A photocopy or fax may be notarized as long as the signature on it is original, meaning that the photocopy or fax must have been signed with pen and ink. Signatures on documents presented for notarization must always be signed with a handwritten, original signature. A photocopied or faxed signature may never be notarized.

Public recorders sometimes will not accept notarized photocopies or faxes, because the text of the document may be too faint to adequately reproduce in microfilming.

Disqualifying Interest

Impartiality. Notaries are appointed by the state to be impartial, disinterested witnesses whose screening duties help ensure the integrity of important legal and commercial transactions. Lack of impartiality by a Notary throws doubt on the integrity and lawfulness of any transaction. A Notary should never notarize his or her own signature, or notarize a document to which the Notary is a party or in which the Notary has any financial or beneficial interest.

Financial or Beneficial Interest. A financial or beneficial interest exists when the Notary is individually named as a principal in a financial transaction or when the Notary receives an advantage, right, privilege, property, or fee valued in excess of the lawfully prescribed Notary fee.

In regard to real estate transactions, a Notary usually is considered to have a disqualifying financial or beneficial interest when that Notary is a grantor or grantee, a mortgagor or mortgagee, a trustor or trustee, a vendor or vendee, a lessor or lessee, or will benefit in any way from the transaction.

Relatives. Notaries are prohibited from notarizing documents to which the Notary or the Notary's spouse or civil union partner is a party, or in which either of them has a direct beneficial interest. Although New Jersey state law does not expressly prohibit notarizing for other relatives, the National Notary Association and state officials strongly advise against doing so for persons related by blood or marriage. Family matters often involve a financial or other beneficial interest that may not be clear at the time of notarization.

Notarizing for family members also may test the Notary's ability to act impartially. For example, a Notary who is asked to notarize a contract signed by his or her brother might attempt to persuade him to sign or not sign. A sibling is entitled to exert influence, but this is entirely improper for a Notary.

Even if a Notary has no interest in the document and does not attempt to influence the signer, notarizing for a relative could subject the document to a legal challenge if other parties to the transaction allege the Notary could not have acted impartially.

Corporations. A New Jersey Notary who is a stockholder, director, officer, employee, or agent of a bank or other corporation may administer an oath to any other stockholder, director, officer, employee, or agent of the corporation (NJSA 41:2-3.

Reasonable Care

Responsibility. As public servants, Notaries must act responsibly and exercise reasonable care in the performance of their official duties. If a Notary fails to do so, he or she may be subject to a civil suit to recover financial damages caused by the Notary's error or omission.

In general, reasonable care is the degree of concern and attentiveness that a person of normal intelligence and responsibility would exhibit. If a Notary can show a judge or jury that he or she did everything expected of a reasonable person, the judge or jury may be required by law to find the Notary blameless and not liable for damages.

Complying with all pertinent laws is the first rule of reasonable care for a Notary. If there are no statutory guidelines in a given instance, the Notary should go to extremes to use common sense and prudence

Unauthorized Practice of Law

Do Not Assist in Legal Matters. A nonattorney Notary may not give legal advice or accept fees for legal advice. As a ministerial official, the nonattorney Notary generally is not permitted to assist a signer in drafting, preparing, selecting, completing, or understanding a document or transaction.

The Notary should not fill in the blank spaces in the text of a document for other persons, tell others what documents they need or how to draft them, nor advise others about the legal sufficiency of a document — and especially not for a fee.

A Notary, of course, may fill in the blanks on the portion of any document containing the Notary certificate. And a Notary, as a private individual, may prepare legal documents that he or she is personally a party to, but the Notary may not notarize his or her own signature on these same documents.

Do Not Determine Notarial Act. A Notary who is not an attorney may not determine the type of notarial act to perform or decide which type of Notary certificate to attach. This is beyond the scope of the Notary's expertise and might be considered the unauthorized practice of law. The Notary should only follow instructions provided by the document, its signer, its issuing or receiving agency, or an attorney.

Exceptions. Specially trained, nonattorney Notaries certified or licensed in a particular field (e.g., real estate, insurance, escrow, etc.) may offer advice or prepare documents related to that field only. Paralegals under the supervision of an attorney may give advice about documents in routine legal matters.

State Treasurer to Take Action. State Treasurer may take action against the commission of a Notary who is not an attorney licensed to practice law, for

a. giving legal advice,

b. acting as an immigration consultant or an expert on immigration matters,

c. otherwise performing the duties of an attorney licensed to practice law in New Jersey, or

d. a disciplinary or other administrative action resulting in a finding of culpability if the applicant holds any professional license regulated by New Jersey, or creating or reinforcing, by any means, a false impression that the person is licensed to engage in the practice of law in New Jersey or any other state, including, but not limited to, committing a violation of NJSA 2C:21-22 or 2C:21-31.

Authentication

Documents Sent Out of State. Documents notarized in New Jersey and sent to other states may be required by the entity receiving the document to bear written proof that the Notary's signature and seal (if used) are genuine and that the Notary had authority to act at the time of notarization. This process of proving the genuineness of an official signature and seal is called authentication or legalization.

In New Jersey, the proof is in the form of an authentication certificate attached to the notarized document by either the county clerk's office where the Notary's signature and certificate of official character are filed or the New Jersey State Treasurer's office.

The county clerk is restricted to providing authentication certificates only to Notaries residing — or working, in the case of nonresidents — in their counties, or to Notaries who have filed copies of their certificate of commission and qualification in their counties. The State Treasurer is authorized to issue authentication certificates relating to any Notary in the state, regardless of where the Notary has filed copies of the commission and qualification certificate (NJSA 52:7-15, 52:7-16).

Authentication certificates are known by different names: certificates of authority, certificates of capacity, certificates of authenticity, certificates of prothonotary, and "flags."

Procedure. It is not the Notary's responsibility to request an authentication certificate for a signer's notarized document. The individual seeking to obtain an authentication certificate must include a cover letter indicating the quantity of documents requiring authentication, along with the notarized documents, and the name, address, and telephone number of the person making the request. The request should be sent or presented to either the clerk of the county in which the Notary has filed the original or a copy of the certificate of commission and qualification or the State Treasurer's office.

For requests sent or presented to the state, the individual seeking an authentication may use the following information:

Mailing address:

> State of New Jersey
> Department of the Treasury
> Division of Revenue and Enterprise Services
> Notary Public Section
> P.O. Box 452 Trenton, NJ 08646

Physical address (for in-person service):

> State of New Jersey
> Department of the Treasury
> Division of Revenue and Enterprise Services
> Notary Public Section
> 33 West State Street, 5th Fl. Trenton, NJ 08608-1214

Telephone: (609) 292-9292

Fees. The State Treasurer charges $25 per document for service via mail ($5 for documents relating to an adoption). Expedited service is available for an additional $15 per document. Payment should be made by check or money order payable to the "Treasurer, State of New Jersey." If requesting authentication from a county, the individual should contact the county clerk for the fee in the particular county.

Documents Sent Out of Country. If the notarized document is going out of the United States, a chain authentication process may be necessary. Additional authentication certificates may have to be obtained from the U.S. Department of State in Washington, D.C., a foreign consulate in Washington, D.C. and a ministry of foreign affairs in the particular foreign nation.

***Apostilles* and The Hague Convention.** More than 100 nations, including the United States, subscribe to a treaty under the auspices of The Hague Conference that simplifies authentication of notarized documents exchanged between any of these nations.

Under this Hague Convention, only one authentication certificate called an apostille is necessary to ensure acceptance in these subscribing countries. (*Apostille* is French for "notation.") It is not necessary to obtain an authentication certificate from the county prior to requesting an *apostille*.

In New Jersey, *apostilles* are issued by the State Treasurer's office (described above). *Apostilles* are not available from the county clerk.

An *apostille* must be specifically requested in writing, including the name, address, and telephone number of the person making the request. The letter also must identify the nation to which the document will be sent. The person requesting the *apostille* must send the letter, the notarized document, and the appropriate fee to the State Treasurer's office.

It should be noted that it is not the Notary's responsibility to obtain an *apostille*. It is the responsibility of the party sending the document out of the country

Foreign Languages

Foreign Language Documents. While New Jersey law does not directly address notarizing documents written in a language the Notary cannot read, it does set restrictions on the recording of documents written in a language other than English.

Any document conveying title to real property that is presented for recording in a county office must be completely in English, including the Notary certificate and any authentication certificates. (Proper names may be in a foreign language, as long as the letters used are those of the English language.) A non-English language conveyance may only be recorded if accompanied by a duly certified English-language translation.

As for notarizing other types of documents written in a language the Notary cannot read, while it is not expressly prohibited, there are difficulties and dangers in doing so.

The foremost danger is that the document may have been misrepresented to the Notary. Blatant fraud might remain undetected, the Notary's act might be misinterpreted in another country, and making a journal entry might be difficult.

Ideally, a foreign-language document should be referred to a Notary who reads that language. In many states, the website of the Notary-regulating official has a Notary directory. These directories often include the foreign languages read or spoken by each Notary listed.

If a Notary chooses to notarize a document that he or she cannot read, then the Notary certificate should be in English or in a language the Notary can read, and the signature being notarized should be written in characters the Notary is familiar with.

Immigration

Do Not Give Advice. Nonattorney Notaries may never advise others on the subject of immigration, nor help others prepare immigration documents — and especially not for a fee. Notaries who offer immigration advice to others may be subject to penalties for the unauthorized practice of law.

Immigration Consultant. An immigration consultant renders non-legal services such as the completion of forms and applications, to determine or modify an individual's immigration or naturalization status under federal law.

An immigration consultant who is not licensed to practice law is guilty of a crime of the third degree if he or she uses or advertises any title, either in English or another language, which means or implies that the immigration consultant is licensed to practice law in New Jersey or any other jurisdiction of the United States (NJSA 2C:21-31).

Wills

Do Not Offer Advice. A Notary risks prosecution for the unauthorized practice of law in advising a signer how to proceed with a will. In addition, the Notary's ill-informed advice may adversely affect the affairs of the signer. The format of a will is dictated by strict laws of each state, and any deviation may result in nullification. In some cases, holographic (handwritten) wills have been voided by notarization.

A Notary should notarize a document described as a will only if a Notary certificate is provided or stipulated for each signer and the signers are not asking questions about how to proceed. Any such questions should be answered by an attorney.

Living Wills. Documents popularly called "living wills" may be notarized. These are not actual wills, but written statements of a signer's wishes concerning medical treatment in the event he or she is unable to issue instructions on his or her own behalf.

Self-Proved Wills. In New Jersey, self-proving wills may require the signatures of the testator and two witnesses to be notarized (NJSA 3B:3-5).

Advance Directives for Health Care

Purpose. Any individual may execute an advance directive for health care. The directive either must be signed and dated in the presence of two witnesses or must be acknowledged before a Notary Public (NJSA 26:2H-56).

If a Notary is asked to take the acknowledgment of the signer of an advance directive for health care, no special procedures are required. The Notary takes the signer's acnowledgment in the usual manner. ■

Official
Notary Acts

Authorized Acts

Notaries may perform the following official acts:

- **Acknowledgments,** certifying that a signer personally appeared before the Notary, was identified by the Notary, and acknowledged freely signing the document (NJSA 46:14-6.1; see pages 26–28).

- **Affidavits,** involving the administration of an oath or affirmation in conjunction with a person's signed statement (NJSA 41:2-17; see page 29).

- **Depositions,** taking down in writing the spoken words of a person giving testimony, though this act is most often done by skilled court reporters (NJ Rules of Civil Procedure, Rule 4:12, Section 4:12-1; see pages 29–30).

- **Verifications on Oath or Affirmation/Jurats,** as found in affidavits and other sworn documents, certifying that the signer personally appeared before the Notary, was identified by the Notary, signed in the Notary's presence, and took an oath or affirmation from the Notary (NJSA 41:2-17; see pages 30–32).

- **Oaths and Affirmations,** which are solemn promises to a Supreme Being (oaths) or solemn promises on one's own personal honor (affirmations) (NJSA 41:2-1, 41:2-17; see pages 32–34).

- **Signature Witnessings/Attestations,** certifying that the signer personally appeared before the Notary, was positively identified, and signed the document in the presence of the Notary (NJAB 4250; see pages 34–35).

- **Copy Certification,** certifying that a copy of a record or item is a full, true, and accurate transcription or reproduction of the record or item (NJAB 4250; see pages 35–36).

- **Proofs of Execution,** certifying that a subscribing witness personally appeared and swore to the Notary that another person, the principal (the signer named in the document), signed that document (NJSA 46:14-6.1; see pages 36–38).

- **Protests,** certifying that a written promise to pay, such as a bill of exchange, was not honored (NJSA 2A:82-7).

- **Witnessing a Safe Deposit Box Opening,** by a bank or other safe deposit box owner, and certifying related details (NJSA 17:14A-51; see pages 38–39).

Acknowledgments

Definition. An acknowledgment is a notarial act in which a document signer personally appears before a Notary, is identified by the Notary as the person named in the document, and admits (or "acknowledges") to the Notary that he or she signed the document for the purposes stated in it. The signer may be signing as an individual, acting on his or her own behalf, or in a representative capacity, acting on behalf of an entity or another person. When a signer is acting in a representative capacity, the signer also acknowledges that he or she has the proper authority to do so (NJSA 46:14-2.1).

Purpose. Acknowledgments are one of the most common forms of notarization. Typically, they are executed on deeds and other instruments that will be publicly recorded by a county official

(NJSA 46:14-2.1). The primary purpose of an acknowledgment is to positively identify the document signer.

Procedure. In executing an acknowledgment, a Notary certifies three things (NJSA 46:14-2.1):

- The signer *personally appeared* before the Notary on the date and in the county indicated on the Notary certificate.

- The signer was *positively identified* by the Notary through either personal knowledge or satisfactory evidence (see "Identifying Document Signers," page 9).

- The signer *acknowledged* to the Notary that the signature is his or hers and was freely made for the purposes stated in the document. If the document is signed in a representative capacity, the signer also acknowledged that he or she had the proper authority to do so. (If a document is willingly signed in the presence of the Notary, this act can serve just as well as an oral statement of acknowledgment.)

Identification of Acknowledger. In executing an acknowledgment, the Notary must identify the signer through personal knowledge, a credible identifying witness or identification documents. (See "Identifying Document Signers," page 9.)

Witnessing Signature Not Required. For an acknowledgment, the document does not have to be signed in the Notary's presence; however, the signer must appear before the Notary at the time of notarization to acknowledge having signed the document (NJSA 46:14-2.1).

A document could have been signed an hour before, a week before, a year before, etc. — as long as the signer appears before the Notary with the signed document at the time of notarization to admit that the signature is his or her own.

Representative Capacity. When the signer is signing in a representative capacity — that is, on behalf of another person or of a legal entity such as a corporation or partnership — the signer does not need to produce proof of his or her capacity. The signer must, however, verbally acknowledge that he or she has the legal authority to sign on behalf of the other person or the entity (NJSA 46:14-2.1).

Certificate for Acknowledgment. For every acknowledgment, the Notary must complete, sign and stamp an appropriate certificate of acknowledgment (NJSA 46:14-2.1).

The certificate wording may either be preprinted or typed at the end of the document, or appear as an attachment (a "certificate form") that is stapled to the document's signature page (NJSA 2A:82-17, 46:14-2.1).

New Jersey statute provides short form acknowledgment certificate wording that Notaries may use. Following are examples of certificates with basic wording, not prohibiting use of any other appropriate wording:

Acknowledgment by Individual (NJSA 52:7-10.12.a.)

State of _____

County of _____

This record was acknowledged before me on _____ (date) by _____ (name of individual(s)).

(Signature of notarial officer)   (Stamp)

(Title of office)

My commission expires: _____

Acknowledgment in a Representative Capacity (NJSA 52:7-10.12.b.)

State of _____

County of _____

This record was acknowledged before me on _____ (date) by _____ (name of individual(s)) as _____ (type of authority, such as officer or trustee) of _____ (name of party on behalf of whom record was executed).

(Signature of notarial officer)   (Stamp)

(Title of office)

My commission expires: _____

Affidavits

Definition. An affidavit is a signed statement made under oath or affirmation before a Notary or other oath-administering official. The signer of an affidavit is called an affiant.

When taking an affidavit, the Notary must administer the oath or affirmation to the affiant and then complete some form of jurat — the name of the Notary wording for affidavits, depositions, and other sworn statements. (See "Jurats," pages 30–32.)

Purpose. Affidavits are used in and out of court for a variety of purposes, from declaring losses to an insurance company to declaring U.S. citizenship before traveling to a foreign country. If an affidavit is used in a judicial proceeding, only one side in the lawsuit or court case need participate in the execution of the affidavit.

Wording for Affidavit Oath (Affirmation). If no other wording is prescribed in a given instance, a Notary may use the following language in administering an oath (or affirmation) to an affiant:

> Do you solemnly swear that the statements in this document are true to the best of your knowledge and belief, so help you God?
>
> (Do you solemnly affirm that the statements in this document are true to the best of your knowledge and belief?)

For both oath and affirmation, the affiant must respond aloud and affirmatively, with "I do" or similar words. It is traditional for the Notary and the affiant to raise their right hands during the oath or affirmation.

Certificate. Affidavits typically require jurat certificates in some form. (See "Jurats," pages 30–32.)

Depositions

Definition. A deposition is a written transcript of a person's oral statements, which the person then signs and swears to or affirms before a Notary or other oath-administering official. The signer of a deposition is called a deponent.

When taking a deposition, the Notary must administer the oath or affirmation to the deponent and then complete some form of jurat

— the name of the Notary wording for affidavits, depositions, and other sworn statements. (See "Jurats," pages 30–32.)

Purpose. Unlike affidavits, depositions are used only in judicial proceedings. With a deposition, both sides in a lawsuit or court case typically have the opportunity to cross-examine the deponent. Their questions and the deponent's answers are taken down and then transcribed into a written statement.

Procedure. New Jersey law permits any Notary to take a deposition — that is, to transcribe the words spoken aloud by a deponent (NJSA 41:2-1, 41:2-17). This duty, however, is most often executed by Notaries who are trained and certified shorthand reporters, also known as court reporters.

While most Notaries do not have the stenographic skills necessary to transcribe a deponent's words, any Notary is competent to administer an oath or affirmation or to execute a jurat for a deposition.

Wording for Deposition Oath (Affirmation). If no other wording is prescribed in a given instance, a Notary may use the following language in administering an oath (or affirmation) to a deponent:

> Do you solemnly swear that the statements in this document are true to the best of your knowledge and belief, so help you God?
>
> (Do you solemnly affirm that the statements in this document are true to the best of your knowledge and belief?)

For both oath and affirmation, the deponent must respond aloud and affirmatively, with "I do" or similar words. It is traditional for the Notary and the deponent to raise their right hands during the oath or affirmation.

Certificate. Depositions typically require jurat certificates in some form. (See "Jurats," pages 30–32.)

Verifications on Oath or Affirmation/Jurats

Definition. A jurat, also known as a verification on oath or affirmation, is a notarial act in which a document signer personally appears before a Notary, is identified by the Notary, signs his or her statement in front of the Notary, and swears or affirms to the Notary that the contents of the statement are true.

Purpose. When notarizing affidavits, depositions, and other forms of written verification requiring the signer to take an oath or affirmation, the Notary normally executes a jurat. While the purpose of an acknowledgment is to positively identify a document signer, the purpose of a jurat is to compel truthfulness by appealing to the signer's conscience and fear of criminal penalties for perjury.

Procedure. In executing a jurat, a Notary certifies four things:

- The signer *personally appeared* before the Notary on the date and in the county indicated on the certificate.

- The signer was *positively identified* by the Notary through either personal knowledge or satisfactory evidence (see "Identifying Document Signers," page 9).

- The Notary *witnessed the signer sign the document* at the time of notarization.

- The Notary *administered an oath or affirmation* to the signer.

A Notary Public does not execute a jurat by merely asking a person whether or not the signature on an affidavit is that of the signer. An oath or affirmation must be administered and the affixation of the signature observed by the Notary (NJSA 41:2-17).

Identification. In executing a jurat, the Notary must identify the signer through personal knowledge, a credible identifying witness, or identification documents. (See "Identifying Document Signers," page 9.)

Wording for Jurat Oath (Affirmation). If not otherwise prescribed by law, a New Jersey Notary may use the following or similar words to administer an oath (or affirmation) in conjunction with a jurat:

Do you solemnly swear that the statements in this document are true to the best of your knowledge and belief, so help you God?

(Do you solemnly affirm that the statements in this document are true to the best of your knowledge and belief?)

For both oath and affirmation, the signer must respond aloud and affirmatively, with "I do" or similar words. It is traditional for the Notary and the signer to raise their right hands during the oath or affirmation.

Certificate. After administering the oath or affirmation, the Notary must complete a notarial certificate.

New Jersey statute provides the following verification on oath or affirmation certificate wording:

Verification on Oath or Affirmation (NJSA 52:7-10.12.c.)

State of _____

County of _____

Signed and sworn to (or affirmed) before me on _____ (date) by _____ (name of individual(s) making statement).

(Signature of notarial officer)   (Stamp)

(Title of office)

My commission expires: _____

Oaths and Affirmations

Definition. An oath is a solemn, spoken pledge to a Supreme Being. An affirmation is a solemn, spoken pledge on one's own personal honor, with no reference to a Supreme Being. Both are usually a promise of truthfulness or fidelity and have the same legal effect.

Purpose. In taking an oath or affirmation in an official proceeding, a person may be subject to criminal penalties for perjury should he or she fail to be truthful.

An oath or affirmation can be a full-fledged notarial act in its own right, as when giving an oath of office to a public official, or it can be part of the process of notarizing a document (e.g., executing a jurat, or swearing in a credible identifying witness).

A person who objects to taking an oath — pledging to a Supreme Being — may instead be given an affirmation (NJSA 41:1-6).

Personal Appearance Required. An oath or affirmation may not be given over the telephone. The person taking the oath or affirmation must physically appear in front of the Notary.

Wording for Oaths (Affirmations). If not otherwise prescribed by law, a New Jersey Notary may use the following or similar words to administer an oath (or affirmation):

- Oath (affirmation) for affiant signing an affidavit or deponent signing a deposition:

  Do you solemnly swear that the statements in this document are true to the best of your knowledge and belief, so help you God?

  (Do you solemnly affirm that the statements in this document are true to the best of your knowledge and belief?)

- Oath (affirmation) for credible identifying witness:

  Do you solemnly swear that you know the signer truly is the person he/she claims to be, so help you God?

  (Do you solemnly affirm that you know the signer truly is the person he/she claims to be?)

- Oath (affirmation) for subscribing witness:

  Do you solemnly swear that you saw (name of document signer) sign his/ her name to this document and/or that he/she acknowledged to you having executed it for the purposes therein stated, so help you God?

  (Do you solemnly affirm that you saw [name of document signer] sign his/ her name to this document and/or that he/she acknowledged to you having executed it for the purposes therein stated?)

Response Required. The person taking the oath or affirmation must respond by repeating the wording in the first person — "I solemnly swear ..." — or by answering affirmatively with, "I do," "Yes," or similar words. A nod or grunt is not a clear and sufficient response.

Ceremony and Gestures. To impress upon the oath-taker or affirmant the importance of truthfulness, the Notary is encouraged to lend a sense of ceremony and formality to the oath or affirmation. During administration of the oath or affirmation, the Notary and the person taking the oath or affirmation traditionally raise their right hands, though this is not a legal requirement.

Notaries generally have discretion to use words and gestures they feel will most compellingly appeal to the conscience of the oath-taker or affirmant.

Exclusions. Only an individual may take an oath or affirmation. An "artificial person" such as a corporation or a partnership may not take an oath.

In addition, a Notary may not administer an oath or affirmation to himself or herself.

Signature Witnessing or Attestation

Purpose. In a signature witnessing, the Notary determines, either from personal knowledge or satisfactory evidence, that the signature on a document is that of the person appearing before the Notary and named in the document.

Witnessing a signature may be used in circumstances where the date of signing is of crucial importance.

A signature witnessing differs from an acknowledgment in that the party relying upon the document will know that the document was signed on a certain date. A signature witnessing differs from a verification upon oath or affirmation in that the signer is merely signing the document, not vouching that the contents of the document are true.

Procedure. In witnessing or attesting a signature, a Notary certifies three things:

1. The signer *personally appeared* before the Notary on the date and in the county indicated on the Notary certificate.

2. The signer was *positively identified* by the Notary through personal knowledge or other satisfactory evidence.

3. The Notary *watched the signer sign the document* at the time of notarization.

Certificate. The following certificate is provided by New Jersey statute, although other certificates with similar wording are not prohibited:

Witnessing or Attesting a Signature (NJSA 52:7-10.12.d.)

State of _____

County of _____

Signed before me on _____ (date) by _____ (name of individual(s)).

(Signature of notarial officer)   (Stamp)

(Title of office)

My commission expires: _____

Copy Certification

Purpose. New Jersey Notaries now have the authority to certify — or "attest" — that a copy of an original document is a complete and true reproduction of the document that was copied. The Notary's authority to certify copies is limited to documents that are not vital records or public records.

Procedure. The permanent custodian of the original document must present it to the Notary and request a certified copy. The Notary should make or closely supervise the making of the photo-copy to ensure that it is true, exact and unaltered.

Examples of the documents that may be lawfully photocopied and certified by a Notary are: a diploma, a driver's license, a vehicle title, a Social Security card, a medical record, a passport, a bill of sale, a contract or a lease.

Certificate. The following certificate is provided by New Jersey statute, although other certificates with similar wording are not prohibited:

Copy Certification (NJSA 52:7-10.12.e.)

State of _____

County of _____

I certify that this is a true and correct copy of a record in the possession of _____.

Dated _____

(Signature of notarial officer)   (Stamp)

(Title of office)

My commission expires: _____

Proof of Execution by Subscribing Witness

Definition. A proof of execution by subscribing witness is a
notarial act in which a subscribing witness personally appears
before a Notary, is identified by the Notary, and swears or affirms
the following facts to the Notary (NJSA 46:14-2.1):

- The subscribing witness personally knows the person named
  in the document — the absent principal signer, on whose
  behalf the subscribing witness is appearing.

- The subscribing witness watched the principal willingly sign
  ("execute") the document or personally took the principal's
  acknowledgment of having willingly signed.

- At the request of the principal, the subscribing witness signed
  ("subscribed") his or her own name to the document as a witness to its execution.

- The subscribing witness' signature and sworn testimony are
  accepted as the "proof" of the document's execution by the
  absent principal signer.

Purpose. In executing a proof of execution by subscribing witness,
a Notary certifies that the signature of a person who does not
appear before the Notary — the principal signer — is genuine and

was freely made, based on the sworn testimony of another person who does appear — a subscribing (signing) witness (NJSA 46:14-2.1).

Proofs of execution are used when the principal signer is out of town or otherwise unavailable to appear before a Notary.

Because of their high potential for fraudulent abuse, proofs of execution are not universally accepted, though they are legal for the New Jersey Notary to perform.

That said, New Jersey state officials discourage the use of proofs of execution by subscribing witness. This type of notarization should only be used as a last resort and never merely because the principal signer prefers not to take the time to personally appear before a Notary.

In Lieu of Acknowledgment. On recordable documents, a proof of execution by subscribing witness is usually regarded as an acceptable substitute for an acknowledgment.

Identifying Subscribing Witness. New Jersey law does not indicate the means by which a subscribing witness may be identified. However, Notary regulators strongly recommend for subscribing witnesses to be personally known to the Notary since Notaries rely entirely on the word of the subscribing witness to vouch for an absent signer's identity, willingness to sign, and general awareness. The certificate wording provided in the *New Jersey Notary Public Manual* for a proof of execution indicates that either the Notary's personal knowledge or the sworn word of a credible identifying witness is an acceptable form of identification; identification documents (ID cards) do not appear to be an option.

Subscribing Witness Qualifications. The ideal subscribing witness personally knows the principal signer and has no personal beneficial or financial interest in the document or transaction. It would be foolish of the Notary, for example, to rely on the word of a subscribing witness presenting for notarization a power of attorney naming that very witness as attorney in fact.

Oath (Affirmation) for Subscribing Witness. An acceptable oath (or affirmation) for the subscribing witness might be:

Do you solemnly swear that you saw (name of the document signer) sign his/ her name to this document and/or that he/she acknowledged to you having executed it for the purposes therein stated, so help you God?

(Do you solemnly affirm that you saw [name of the document signer] sign his/ her name to this document and/or that he/she acknowledged to you having executed it for the purposes therein stated?)

Certificate for Proof of Execution. New Jersey statute does not prescribe a Notary certificate for a proof of execution by subscribing witness, though it does specify that the witness must swear that he or she saw the principal signer execute the document (NJSA 46:14-2.1). The National Notary Association recommends the following wording:

State of New Jersey)

) ss.

County of _____)

On _____ (date), before me, _____, Notary Public in and for said county, personally appeared _____ (name[s] of subscribing witness[es]), personally known to me (or proved to me on the oath of _____ [name of credible identifying witness]) to be the person(s) whose name(s) is/are subscribed on the attached document as witness(es) thereto, and who, being duly sworn by me, say(s) that he/she/they saw _____ (name of absent principal) sign the attached document, and that said affiant(s) subscribed his/her/their name(s) to the attached document at the request of _____ (name of absent principal).

Notary's Signature _____ (Notary's Seal)

Witnessing Safe Deposit Box Opening

Purpose. If the rental fee on a safe deposit box, vault, or receptacle has not been paid for one year, and the bank or safe deposit box owner has attempted to contact the lessee without success, the bank may open and inventory the box in the presence of a Notary Public and one of the institution's officers.

Procedure. The Notary issues a certificate stating the lessee's name, the date of the opening, and a list of the contents in the box. The Notary then delivers the certificate to the institution. Within 10 days of the opening, a copy of the certificate must be mailed by the owner of the safe deposit box to the lessee's last known address (NJSA 17:14A-51).

Certificate for Inventorying a Safe Deposit Box. New Jersey law does not provide specific wording for the certificate. The National Notary Association recommends the following wording:

State of New Jersey   )

) ss.

County of _____)

On the _____ (day) of _____ (month), _____
(year), safe deposit box number _____, rented in the name
of _____, was opened by _____
(name of financial institution) in my presence and in the presence
of _____ (name of financial institution officer). The
contents of the box consisted of the following: (list of contents)

_____ (Signature of financial institution officer)

_____ (Print or type name)

_____ (Signature of Notary)   (Notary's Seal)

_____ (Name of Notary, printed, typed or stamped)

Fees for Notary Services

Maximum Fees. The following maximum fees for performing notarial acts are allowed by New Jersey law (NJSA 22A:4-14):

- **Acknowledgments — $2.50.** For taking an acknowledgment, the fee is not to exceed $2.50 per signature.

- **Oaths and Affirmations — $2.50.** For administering an oath or affirmation or taking an affidavit, with or without a jurat certificate, the fee is not to exceed $2.50 per person or signer.

- **Jurats — $2.50.** For executing a jurat with an oath or

affirmation, the fee is not to exceed the fee allowed for an oath or affidavit, $2.50 per signer.

- **Proofs of Execution by Subscribing Witness — $2.50.** For taking a proof of execution by subscribing witness, the maximum fee is the same as for an acknowledgment, $2.50 per signature.

- **Real Estate Transfer.** In performing any of the above notarizations for a real estate transfer, regardless of the number of notarizations performed in the transaction, a Notary may charge $15.

- **Financing of Real Estate.** In performing notarizations for mortgagors in the financing of a real estate transaction, regardless of the number of notarizations performed in the transaction, a Notary may charge $25.

- **Protests — $2.** For executing a protest, the fee is not to exceed $2. For each additional notice of protest delivered in person or by mail, a Notary may charge $0.10 in addition to postage fees.

Fee Schedule May Change. The New Jersey Assembly Bill 4250 states that for administering oaths, taking affidavits, taking proofs of a deed, and taking acknowledgments, Notaries, judges, and other officers authorized by law to perform such services shall receive a fee as fixed by the State Treasurer by regulation. Until the new maximum fees are set, Notaries should continue to charge reasonable fees consistent with that which is currently prescribed.

Record Fees. The new laws require the Notary to itemize all fees charged for notarial services in the Notary's journal. (NJAB 4250)

Travel Fees. Charges for travel by a Notary are not specified by law. Such fees are allowed only if the Notary and signer should agree beforehand on the amount to be charged. The signer must understand that a travel fee is not stipulated in law and is separate from the Notary fees described above.

Option Not to Charge. Notaries are not required to charge for their Notary services, and they may charge any fee less than the maximum.

Overcharging. For charging more than the legally prescribed fees in executing a protest, a court may demand a Notary pay $25 for each violation to the person overcharged (NJSA 22A:4-13).

Although the laws only prescribe penalties for protests, charging more than the maximum statutory fee for any notarial act may subject the Notary to penalties or charges of discrimination.

Advertising

False or Misleading Advertising. A Notary's commission may be revoked or suspended if the Notary advertises or claims to have powers not authorized by law. For example, Notaries may not advertise that they have the authority to officially certify the translation of a document, since this is not a power given by New Jersey law.

Effective December 8, 2014, Notaries advertising their services, in either English or another language, must include the following notice in the advertisement: "I am not an attorney licensed to practice law and may not give legal advice about immigration or any other legal matter or accept fees for legal advice" (NJSA 52:7-11, 52:7-14, 52:7-17).

For practicing fraud or deceit in advertising or any other activity as a Notary, the Notary may be found guilty of a crime of the second degree or above (NJSA 57:7-20, 57:7-21). ▪

Recordkeeping

Journal of Notarial Acts

Required. New Jersey requires a Notary to maintain a journal of all notarial acts the Notary performs.

Format. The journal may be created and maintained on a tangible medium or in an electronic format. If the journal is maintained on a tangible medium, it must be a permanent, bound register with consecutively numbered lines and consecutively numbered pages. If the journal is maintained in an electronic format, it must be in a permanent, tamper-evident electronic format complying with any rules and regulations promulgated by the State Treasurer in the *New Jersey Notary Public Manual.*

A Notary must maintain only one journal at a time to chronicle all notarial acts, whether those notarial acts are performed regarding tangible or electronic records.

Purpose. Prudent Notaries keep detailed and accurate journals of their notarial acts for many reasons:

- Keeping records is a *businesslike practice* in which every conscientious Notary and public official should engage.

- A Notary's recordbook *protects the public's rights* to valuable property and to due process by providing documentary evidence in the event a document is lost or altered, or if a transaction is later challenged.

- In the event of a civil lawsuit alleging that the Notary's negligence or misconduct caused the plaintiff serious financial harm, a detailed journal of notarial acts can *protect the Notary* by showing that reasonable care was used to identify a signer. It would be difficult to contend that the Notary did not bother to identify a signer if the Notary's journal contains a detailed description of the ID cards that the signer presented.

Journal Entries. The Notary's journal must contain the following information for each notarial act performed (NJSA 52:7-10.18.b):

a. the date and time of the notarial act;

b. the type of notarial act, including but not limited to the taking of an acknowledgment, the administration of an oath, or the taking of an affidavit;

c. the name and address of each person for whom the notarial act is performed;

d. if the identity of the individual is based on personal knowledge, a statement to that effect;

e. if the identity of the individual is based on satisfactory evidence, a brief description of the method of identification and the identification credential presented, if any, including, if applicable, the type, date of issuance, and date of expiration of an identification document, or the name and signature of any identifying witness and, if applicable, the type, date of issuance, and date of expiration of a document identifying the witness; and

f. an itemized list of all fees charged for the notarial act.

Document Description. Recording the title or a description of the document will be helpful if there are future questions regarding the nature of the document that was notarized. If the document has a specific date on it, the Notary should record that date in the journal of notarial acts, too.

Often the only date on a document is the date of the signature that is being notarized. If the signature is undated, however, the document may have no date on it at all. In that case, the Notary should record "no date" or "undated" in the journal.

For acknowledgments, the date the document was signed must either precede or be the same as the date of the notarization; it may not follow it. For a jurat, the date the document was signed and the date of the notarization must be the same.

A document whose signature is dated after the date on its Notary certificate risks rejection by a recorder, who may question how the document could have been notarized before it was signed.

Journal Signature. Another important entry to obtain is the signer's signature. A journal signature protects the Notary against claims that a signer did not appear and is a deterrent to forgery, because it provides evidence of the signer's identity and appearance before the Notary.

To check for possible forgery, the Notary should compare the signature that the person leaves in the journal of notarial acts with the signatures on the document and on the IDs. The signatures should be at least reasonably similar.

The Notary also should observe the signing of the journal. If the signer appears to be laboring over the journal signature, this may be an indication of forgery in progress.

Since a journal signature is not required by law, the Notary may not refuse to notarize if the signer declines to leave one.

Additional Entries. Notaries may include additional information in the journal that is pertinent to a given notarization. Many Notaries, for example, enter the telephone number of all signers and witnesses, as well as the address where the notarization was performed, if not at the Notary's office. A description of the document signer's demeanor (e.g., "The signer appeared very nervous") or notations about the identity of other persons who were present for the notarization may also be pertinent.

One important entry to include is the signer's representative capacity — whether the signer is acting as attorney in fact, trustee, guardian, corporate officer, or in another capacity — if not signing on his or her own behalf.

Complete Entry Before Certificate. The prudent Notary completes the journal entry before filling out the Notary certificate on a document. This prevents the signer from leaving with the notarized document before vital information can be entered in the journal.

Never Surrender Journal. Notaries should never surrender control of their journals to anyone, unless expressly subpoenaed by a court order. Even when an employer has paid for the Notary's official journal, it goes with the Notary upon termination of employment.

No person but the Notary may properly possess and use this official tool of the Notary's office. This also means that a Notary may never share his or her journal with another person, even if the other person also is a Notary.

Disposition of Journal. The Notary must either retain the journal for 10 years after the performance of the last notarial act recorded in the journal or transmit the journal to the Department of the Treasury, Division of Revenue and Enterprise Services, or a repository approved by the State Treasurer (NJSA 52:7-10.18.d).

On resignation from, or the revocation or suspension of, a Notary's commission, the Notary must either:

a.   retain the journal for 10 years after the performance of the last notarial act recorded in the journal and inform the State Treasurer where the journal is located; or

b.   ransmit the journal to the Department of the Treasury, Division of Revenue and Enterprise Services, or a repository approved by the State Treasurer (NJAC 17:50-1.11[e]).

On the death or adjudication of incompetency of a current or former Notary, the Notary's personal representative or guardian or any other person knowingly in possession of the journal must, within 45 days, transmit it to the Department of the Treasury, Division of Revenue and Enterprise Services, or a repository approved by the State Treasurer (NJSA 52:7-10.18.f).

Lost or Stolen Journal. If a Notary's journal is lost or stolen, the Notary must notify the State Treasurer within 10 days of the loss or theft (NJAC 17:50-1.11[c]).

Attorney Exception. In lieu of maintaining a journal, a Notary who is an attorney-at-law admitted to practice in New Jersey, or who is employed by an attorney-at-law, or who is employed by or acting as an agent for a title insurance company licensed to do business in New Jersey pursuant NJSA 17:22A-26 et seq., is authorized to maintain a record of notarial acts in the form of files regularly maintained for the attorney's law practice or the title insurance company's business activities, as the case may be. ▪

Notary Certificate and Seal

Notary Certificate

Definition. The Notary certificate is wording that indicates exactly what the Notary has certified or attested to in a particular notarization.

Requirement. When notarizing any document, a Notary must complete a Notary certificate (NJSA 2A:82-17 and 41:2-17).

Completing the Certificate. The Notary certificate either may be preprinted or typed on the document itself or may be an attachment to it. The certificate must (52:7-19.a):

a. be executed contemporaneously with the performance of the notarial act;

b. be signed and dated by the Notary;

c. identify the jurisdiction in which the notarial act is performed; and

d. indicate the date of expiration of the Notary's commission.

The certificate must also state (NJSA 46:14-2.1.c):

a. that the maker or the witness personally appeared before the Notary;

b. that the Notary was satisfied that the person who made the acknowledgment or proof was the maker of or the witness to the instrument;

c. the Notary's name and title; and

d. the date on which the acknowledgment was taken

Correcting a Certificate. When filling out the certificate, the Notary should make sure any preprinted information is accurate. For example, the venue — the state and county in which the notarial act is taking place — may have been filled in prior to the notarization. If the preprinted venue is incorrect, the Notary must line through the incorrect state and/or county, write in the proper site of the notarization, and initial and date the change.

When certificate wording is not preprinted on the document, or when preprinted wording is not acceptable, the Notary may attach a certificate form. This form typically is stapled to the document's left margin following the signature page.

If the certificate form is replacing unacceptable preprinted wording, the Notary should line through the preprinted wording and write below it, "See attached certificate." If the document has no preprinted wording, however, the Notary should not add this notation. Those words could be viewed as an unauthorized change to the document.

To prevent a certificate form from being removed and fraudulently placed on another document, the Notary may add a brief description of the document to the certificate: "This certificate is attached to a _____ (title or type of document), dated _____ (date), of _____ (number) pages, signed by _____ (name[s] of signer[s])."

While fraud-deterrent steps such as these can make it much more difficult for a certificate form to be removed and misused, there is no absolute protection against its removal and misuse. While a certificate form remains in their control, however, Notaries must absolutely ensure that it is attached only to its intended document.

Selecting Certificates. Nonattorney Notaries should never select Notary certificates for any transaction. It is not the role of a nonattorney Notary to decide what type of certificate — and thus what type of notarization — a document needs. As ministerial officials, Notaries generally follow instructions and complete forms that have been provided for them; they do not issue instructions or decide which forms are appropriate in a given case.

If a document is presented to a Notary without certificate wording and if the signer does not know what type of notarial act is appropriate, the signer should be asked to find out what kind of notarization and certificate are needed. Usually the agency that issued or will be accepting the document can provide this information. A Notary who selects certificates may be engaging in the unauthorized practice of law.

Do Not Pre-Sign or Pre-Seal Certificates. A Notary must never sign and/or seal certificates ahead of time or permit other persons to attach certificate forms to documents.

These actions could facilitate fraud or forgery, and they could subject the Notary to lawsuits to recover damages resulting from the Notary's neglect or misconduct.

False Certificates. A Notary who knowingly completes a false Notary certificate may be subject to criminal penalties. A Notary would be completing a false certificate, for example, if he or she signed and sealed an acknowledgment certificate indicating a signer personally appeared when the signer actually did not.

Notaries may be pressured by employers, clients, friends or relatives to be untruthful in their official certificates. If a Notary complies with these requests, he or she may be convicted of a crime of dishonesty. A New Jersey Notary who is convicted of such crimes may lose his or her Notary commission or be denied any future commission. The Notary may also be subject to a civil lawsuit and damages brought by the injured party (NJSA 52:7-20, 52:7-21).

Notary Seal

Required. New Jersey law requires a Notary to use an official stamp on a tangible and electronic record. It must be capable of being copied together with the record to which it is affixed or attached or with which it is logically associated (NJSA 52:7-10.5.b).

Required Information. The official stamp must include the name of the Notary, the title "Notary Public, State of New Jersey", and the Notary's commission expiration date (NJSA 52:7-10.5.a).

Embossing and Inking Seals. There are two types of Notary seals: the metal embosser, which crimps its impression onto a paper surface and aids in distinguishing photocopies from originals; and the inked stamp, usually with a rubber face, which imprints a photocopiable impression on the paper. Since the seal impression must be photographically reproducible, if a Notary uses an embosser as the official seal, it would need to be inked.

Placement of Seal or Stamp Impression. The Notary's official seal should be placed near but not over the Notary's signature on the Notary certificate.

If there is no room for the seal or stamp, the Notary may have no choice but to complete and attach a certificate form that duplicates the notarial wording on the document.

If the Notary cannot physically use the stamping device, the Notary may authorize and provide specific instruction to another person to affix the stamping device for the Notary (NJSA 52:7-10.6.a).

L.S. On many certificates the letters "L.S." appear, indicating where the seal is to be located. These letters abbreviate the Latin term *locus sigilli*, meaning "place of the seal." An inking seal should be placed near but not over the letters, so that wording imprinted by the seal will not be obscured.

Illegible Seal. If an initial seal impression is unreadable and there is ample room on the document, another impression can be affixed nearby. The illegibility of the first impression will indicate why a second seal impression was necessary. The Notary should then record in the journal that a second impression was applied.

A Notary should never attempt to fix an imperfect seal impression with pen, ink or correction fluid. This may be viewed as evidence of tampering and cause the document to be rejected by a receiving agency.

Never Surrender Seal. Notaries must never surrender control of their seals to anyone. Even when an employer has paid for the Notary's official seal, it goes with the Notary upon termination of employment. No person but the Notary may properly possess and use this official tool of the Notary's office. This also means that a Notary may not share his or her seal with another person, even if the other person also is a Notary.

Lost or Stolen Seal. If the stamping device used by the Notary is lost or stolen, the Notary or the Notary's personal representative must notify the State Treasurer of the loss or theft within 10 days (NJAC 17:50-1.8[l]). ▨

In-Person Electronic Notarization and Remote Notarization

Purpose. Electronic commerce produces a need for Notaries to witness electronic transactions, just as Notaries have witnessed paper transactions for centuries. While the tools for creating and signing documents may be different, the impartial witnessing services of a Notary remain the same and are as important as ever. In this chapter, you can review the various types of electronic and remote notarization processes and the statutes that have been set forth thus far.

In-Person Electronic Notarization. In-person electronic notarization, also called IPEN or eNotarizations, still requires the Notary and signer to meet face-to-face and be physically in the same room. Similar to pen and paper notarizations, the Notary must identify the signer through personal knowledge or satisfactory evidence, screen the signer for willingness and awareness, and certify the facts for the requested notarization. However, for electronic notarizations, the document is presented electronically, such as on a computer or tablet, and the signature will be affixed electronically by the signer. The notary certificate will be provided at the end of the document or logically attached to the document for the Notary to complete and affix the electronic signature and the electronic seal. And of course, a journal record is made.

Remote Online Notarization. When the Notary and signer cannot meet face-to-face in the same room, a remote online notarization, also referred to as a RON, can be performed. RON requires the Notary and signer to meet via audio-video technology that allows them to see and hear each other in real-time. The electronic record or document and the electronic Notary certificate are uploaded to a shared platform by a Notary technology provider, and the notarization takes place via that platform. The Notary would still follow the fundamental steps for the notarization. The Notary screens the signer for identity, willingness and awareness and certifies the facts for the requested notarization. Then the Notary completes the electronic certificate and affixes an electronic signature and seal. A journal record is made, along with an audio-video recording of the transaction. A remote online notarization may not be performed on a record relating to the creation and execution of a will or codicil.

Remote Ink-Signed Notarization. Another option when notarizing for a remotely located individual is remote ink-signed notarization, sometimes referred to as RIN. RIN authorizes a Notary in New Jersey to use communication technology to take an acknowledgment of a signature on a tangible record (including a record that relates to a law governing the creation and execution of wills or codicils) that is in the possession of the Notary if the record is displayed to and identified by the remotely located individual during the audio-visual session. As with all acknowledgments, the Notary screens the signer for identity, willingness and awareness and then takes the acknowledgment of the individual, but for RIN transactions, this is accomplished using audio-video communication technology. The document is then sent to the Notary for completion of the tangible notarial certificate, using a wet signature and traditional stamp. A journal record is made, along with an audio-video recording of the transaction.

Authorization for Remote Notarizations. A Notary must notify the State Treasurer that the Notary will be performing notarial acts for remotely located individuals before the Notary's first such act and inform the State Treasurer of the technologies the Notary will be using. Procedures for authorization as well as required technologies will be established by the State Treasurer.

Location of Remote Individual. For RON and RIN, the remotely located individual may be physically located anywhere and not just in New Jersey. For a remotely located individual located outside the United States, the record must be intended to be filed with or relate to a matter before a public official or court, governmental entity, or other entity subject to the jurisdiction of the United States; or involve property located in the territorial jurisdiction of the United States or involve a transaction substantially connected with the United States. Moreover, the act of making the statement or signing the record must not be prohibited by the foreign state in which the remotely located individual is located.

Verification of the Record to be Notarized. For any remote notarization transaction, the Notary must be able to reasonably confirm that a record presented to the Notary is the same record in which the remotely located individual made a statement or on which the individual executed a signature.

Identification of the Remotely Located Individual. The Notary must identify a remotely located individual by personal knowledge, a credible witness appearing physically or using communication technology to appear before the notarial officer, or by satisfactory evidence using at least two different types of identity proofing. Typically, the technology provider will implement identity proofing even if the Notary personally knows the signer or uses a credible witness. Identity proofing is accomplished by analyzing the signer's ID through credential analysis software and asking the signer to answer knowledge-based authentication questions.

1. **Credential Analysis** is the process by which the government-issued identification card of the principal is validated. The process requires a third party to use technology confirming the security features on an ID and that the ID is not fraudulent. The third party also uses information available from the issuing source or other authoritative source to confirm the details on the credential. As part of the process, the third party is required to provide an output of the authenticity test to the Notary and enable the Notary to visually

compare the credential used during credential analysis with the principal who has personally appeared before the Notary via audio-visual transmission.

2. **Knowledge Based Authentication** is a method of authentication which seeks to prove the identity of someone accessing a service such as a financial institution or website. As the name suggests, Knowledge Based Authentication requires the knowledge of private information of the individual to prove that the person providing the identity information is the owner of the identity. There are two types of KBA: Static KBA, which is based on a pre-agreed set of shared secrets, and Dynamic KBA, which is based on questions generated from a wider base of personal information.

Record Notarization. In addition to recording a journal entry as required for traditional notarizations, the Notary, or person acting on behalf of the Notary, must create an audio-visual recording of the performance of the notarial act. Unless a different period is required by rule, the recording should be retained for a period of at least 10 years after the recording is made.

Notary Certificate. A Notary certificate for a remotely located individual must indicate that the notarial act was performed using communication technology. The New Jersey prescribed short form certificate is sufficient for a notarial act involving communication technology if it:

a. complies with any rules or regulations adopted by the State Treasurer or;

b. is in the form provided by Section 21 of the Act and contains a statement substantially as follows: "This notarial act involved the use of communication technology."

Specific Rules for Remote Ink-Signed Notarizations

Emergency Rules Become Permanent. New Jersey is the first state to adopt the 2021 amendments to the RULONA that explicitly authorize notarial acts for remotely located individuals on tangible (paper) records. NJAB 4250 makes many of the Covid emergency rules of NJAB 3903 permanent and authorizes a Notary to use communication technology to take an acknowledgment of a signature on a tangible record (including a record that relates to a law governing the creation and execution of wills or codicils) that is in the possession of the Notary if the record is displayed to and identified by the remotely located individual during an audio-visual session. The rules and provisions established by NJAB 3903 and carried over into NJAB 4250 are provided below:

Confirm Record. The Notary must reasonably confirm that the tangible record (including a record that relates to a law governing the creation and execution of wills or codicils) before the officer is the same record in which the remotely located individual made a statement or on which the individual executed a signature. This requirement is satisfied if the individual signs the record and a declaration which is part of or securely attached to the record during the audio-visual session.

Required Declaration. The required declaration must substantially read as follows: "I declare under penalty of perjury that the record to which this declaration is attached is the same record on which [name of notarial officer] performed a notarial act and before whom I appeared by means of communication technology on [date]" and contain the printed and signed name of the remotely located individual.

The remotely located individual for whom the Notary performs a notarial act on a tangible record using communication technology is required to send the record and declaration to the officer not later than 3 days after the notarial act was performed.

Identification of the Remotely Located Individual. The Notary must identify a remotely located individual by personal knowledge, a credible witness appearing physically or using communication technology to appear before the notarial officer, or by satisfactory evidence using at least two different types of identity proofing as described above.

Journal and Audio-Video Recording. As with RON transactions, the Notary must record a journal entry and capture the remotely located individual signing the tangible record and required declaration in the audio-visual recording of the notarial act.

Complete the Notary Certificate. After receipt of the record and declaration from the individual, the Notary must execute the Notary certificate, which must include the following statement or words of similar import, "I [name of notarial officer] witnessed, by means of communication technology [name of remotely located individual] sign the attached record and date on [date]." ■

Misconduct and Penalties

Denial, Revocation, Suspension, or Limitation. The State Treasurer may deny a Notary commission, refuse to renew, suspend, revoke, or limit the commission for any act or omission that shows the individual lacks the honesty, integrity, competence, or reliability necessary to act as a Notary, including but not limited to:

Application Misstatement. A fraudulent, dishonest, or deceitful misstatement or omission in the Notary application.

Fraud, Dishonesty, Deceit. A finding against or admission of liability in any legal proceeding or disciplinary action based on fraud, dishonesty, or deceit.

Conviction of a Crime. A conviction of a crime of the second degree or above.

Failure to Discharge Duties. Failure by the notary public to discharge any duty required by any law.

False or Misleading Advertising. Use of false or misleading advertising or representation.

Failure to Take Oath of Office. Failure to take the Notary Public oath within three months of the receipt of commission.

Withholding a Record. Withholding access to or possession of an original record or photocopy provided by a person who seeks performance of a notarial act except where allowed by law.

Notary Limitation in Another State. The denial of an application for Notary in another state; the refusal to renew in another state; or the suspension, revocation, or other limitation of the commission of the Notary in another state.

Unauthorized Practice of Law. In the case of a non-attorney Notary, the unauthorized practice of law includes any of the following:

1.   Giving legal advice;

2.   Acting as an immigration consultant or an expert on immigration matters;

3.   Otherwise performing the duties of an attorney licensed to practice law in New Jersey;

4.   A disciplinary or other administrative action resulting in a finding of culpability if the applicant holds any professional license regulated by the State; or

5.   Creating or reinforcing, by any means, a false impression that the person is licensed to engage in the practice of law in New Jersey or any other state.

Failure to Comply with State Notary Laws. Failure to comply with New Jersey Laws on Notarial Acts (N.J.S.A. 52:7-10).

Right to Respond to Charges

Administrative Action Against Notary. Before the State Treasurer takes action against a commission, the accused Notary usually has a chance to respond to the charges. If there is no response from the accused Notary, the State Treasurer will take appropriate action. ■

New Jersey Laws Pertaining to Notaries Public

Reprinted on the following pages are pertinent sections of the New Jersey Statutes Annotated (NJSA) affecting Notaries and notarial acts. These statutes, along with this *Primer*, should be studied thoroughly before executing any notarial acts.

Citations at the end of each section indicate the most recent legislative action on the particular section. Three asterisks (***) in the text of a section indicate that irrelevant material has been omitted by the National Notary Association editors.

NOTE: Pursuant to the authority of the Executive Reorganization Act (NJSA 52:14C-1, et. seq.), all functions of the Division of Commercial Recording — which includes the Notary Public Section — have been transferred from the Secretary of State to the Department of the Treasury.

NEW JERSEY STATUTES ANNOTATED

TITLE 2A. ADMINISTRATION OF CIVIL AND CRIMINAL JUSTICE
SUBTITLE 9. EVIDENCE
CHAPTER 82. WRITINGS AND RECORDS

ARTICLE 4. NOTARIAL PROTESTS

2A:82-5. Record used to refresh memory

When a notary public or any other person authorized to protest instruments under the laws of this state is called upon to testify concerning a protest made by him, he may, to refresh his memory, refer to the record thereof kept by him as required by law.

L. 1951 (1st SS), c. 344.

§ 2A:82-6. Copies of record of protest as evidence

If it appears that the notary or other officer of this state by whom any bill of exchange or promissory note was protested has died or removed from the state or, after diligent inquiry, his place of residence cannot be discovered, the record deposited in the county clerk's office, as required by section 7:5-5 of the title Bills, Notes and Checks, of the Revised Statutes, or a copy thereof certified by such clerk, shall be received as competent evidence of the matter contained in such record.

When the register or other book of any notary public appointed and qualified under the laws of any state of the United States containing a record of the official acts of such notary public by him done in pursuance of his office is, in pursuance of the law of such state, by reason of the death, removal or other disability of the notary public, deposited in the office of the clerk, prothonotary or recorder of deeds of the city, town or county in which the notary public resided at the time of his acting as notary public, a copy of the record or of any part thereof respecting the protesting of any note or bill of exchange protested by the notary public, and the time when, place where and upon whom demand of acceptance or payment was made, with a copy of the notice of nonacceptance or nonpayment (if a copy of the notice shall appear on said record), how the notice of nonacceptance or nonpayment was served, and the time when, or if sent, in what manner, and the time when, and to whom, duly certified under the hand and seal of such clerk, prothonotary or recorder of deeds, or otherwise proved to be truly taken from said record, shall be held and received in all the courts of this state as competent evidence of the facts therein recited, and also of the official character of the notary public. When it shall appear from such record that the said note or bill of exchange had been protested for want of acceptance or payment thereof, and that the said notary public making such protest had duly notified the drawer or endorsers, by mail, of the demand of payment or acceptance and refusal thereof, without specifying the names or the post office address of such drawer or endorsers, the copy of the record certified or proved as aforesaid, shall be held and received in all courts of this state as competent evidence that the drawer and endorsers of such note or bill of exchange were duly notified of such demand and refusal.

L. 1951 (1st SS), c. 344.

2A:82-7. Certificate of protest as evidence.

The certificate of a notary public of this state or of any other state of the United States, under his hand and official seal accompanying any bill of exchange or promissory note which has been protested by such notary for nonacceptance or nonpayment, shall be received in all the courts of this state as competent evidence of the official character of such notary, and also of the facts therein certified as to the presentment and dishonor of such bill or note and of the time and manner of giving or sending notice of dishonor to the parties to such bill or note.

L.1951 (1st SS), c.344.

2A:82-17. Certificates of acknowledgment or proof of instruments as evidence of execution thereof.

If any instrument heretofore made and executed or hereafter to be made and executed shall have been acknowledged, by any party who shall have executed it, or the execution thereof by such party shall have been proved by one or more of the subscribing witnesses to such instrument, in the manner and before one of the officers provided and required by law for the acknowledgment or proof of instruments in order to entitle them to be recorded, and, when a certificate of such acknowledgment or proof shall be written upon or under, or be annexed to such instrument and signed by such officer in the manner prescribed by law, such certificate of acknowledgment or proof shall be and constitute prima facie evidence of the due execution of such instrument by such party. Such instrument shall be received in evidence in any court or proceeding in this state in the same manner and to the same effect as though the execution of such instrument by such party had been proved by other evidence.

L.1951 (1st SS), c.344.

TITLE 2C. THE NEW JERSEY CODE OF CRIMINAL JUSTICE
SUBTITLE 2. SPECIFIC OFFENSES
PART 4. OFFENSES INVOLVING PUBLIC ADMINISTRATION OFFICIALS
CHAPTER 28. PERJURY AND FALSIFICATION TO AUTHORITIES

2C:28-8. Impersonating a public servant or law enforcement officer.

a. Except as provided in subsection b. of this section, a person commits a disorderly persons offense if he falsely pretends to hold a position in the public service with purpose to induce another to submit to such pretended official authority or otherwise to act in reliance upon that pretense.

b. A person commits a crime of the fourth degree if he falsely pretends to hold a position as an officer or member or employee or agent of any organization or association of law enforcement officers with purpose to induce another to submit to such pretended official authority or otherwise to act in reliance upon that pretense.

L.1978, c.95; amended 2000, c.110.

SUBTITLE 3. SENTENCING
CHAPTER 43. GENERAL PROVISIONS

2C:43-3. Fines and restitution.

A person who has been convicted of an offense may be sentenced to pay a fine, to make restitution, or both, such fine not to exceed: ...

***

c. $1,000.00, when the conviction is of a disorderly persons offense: ...

***

e. Any higher amount equal to double the pecuniary gain to the offender or loss to the victim caused by the conduct constituting the offense by the offender. In such case the court shall make a finding as to the amount of the gain or loss, and if the record does not contain sufficient evidence to support such a finding the court may conduct a hearing upon the issue. For purposes of this section the terms "gain" means the amount of money or the value of property derived by the offender and "loss" means the amount of value separated from the victim. The term "gain" shall also mean, where appropriate, the amount of any tax, fee, penalty, and interest avoided, evaded, or otherwise unpaid or improperly retained or disposed of; ...

***

The restitution ordered paid to the victim shall not exceed his loss, except that in any case involving the failure to pay any State tax, the amount of restitution to the State shall be the full amount of the tax avoided or evaded, including full civil penalties and interest as provided by law. In any case where the victim of the offense is any department or division of State government, the court shall order restitution to the victim. Any restitution imposed on a person shall be in addition to any fine which may be imposed pursuant to this section.

L.1978, c.95; amended 1979, c.178, s.83; 1981, c.290, s.37; 1987, c.76, s.34; 1987, c.106, s.10; 1991, c.329, s.2; 1995, c.20, s.6; 1995, c.417, s.2; 1997, c.181, s.12.

TITLE 12A. COMMERCIAL TRANSACTIONS
SUBTITLE 1. UNIFORM COMMERCIAL CODE
CHAPTER 12. UNIFORM ELECTRONIC TRANSACTIONS

12A:12-11. Notarized signatures or records.

11. If a law requires a signature or record to be notarized, acknowledged, verified, or made under oath, the requirement is satisfied if the electronic signature of the person authorized to perform those acts, together with all other information required to be included by other applicable law, is attached to or logically associated with the signature or record.

L.2001, c.116, s.11.

TITLE 17. CORPORATIONS AND INSTITUTIONS FOR FINANCE AND INSURANCE
SUBTITLE 2. FINANCIAL INSTITUTIONS
PART 3. SAFE DEPOSIT COMPANIES
CHAPTER 14A. SAFE DEPOSIT BUSINESSES

17:14A-51. Proceedings for unpaid rental.

If the amount due for the rental of any vault, safe deposit box or receptacle for the storage and safekeeping of personal property of any safe deposit company or bank, savings bank, or savings and loan association authorized to conduct a safe deposit business under the laws of this State has not been paid for one year, the safe deposit company, bank, savings bank, savings and loan association may at any time after the expiration of the year send a written notice by registered mail addressed to the lessee or lessees in whose name the vault, safe deposit or receptacle stands on its records, directed to the address on its records, that if the rental for the vault, safe deposit box or receptacle is not paid within 30 days after the date of the mailing of the notice, it will have the vault, safe deposit box or receptacle opened in the presence of one of its officers and of a notary public not in its employ, and the contents thereof, if any, placed in a sealed package by the notary public, marked by him with the name of the lessee or lessees in whose name the vault, safe deposit box or receptacle stands and the estimated value thereof, and the package so sealed and marked will be placed in one of the general vaults, safes or boxes of the safe deposit company, bank, savings bank or savings and loan association. The notary's proceedings shall be set forth in a certificate under his official seal, and the certificate shall be delivered to the savings and loan association, bank, savings bank or safe deposit company. The safe deposit company, bank, savings bank or savings and loan association shall have a lien on the contents of the vault, safe deposit box or receptacle so removed for the amount due to it for the rental of the vault, safe deposit box or receptacle up to the time of the removal of the contents, and for the costs and expenses, if any incurred in its opening, repairing and restoration for use. If the lien is not paid and discharged within one year from the opening of the vault, safe deposit box or receptacle and the removal of its contents, the safe deposit company, bank, savings bank or savings and loan association may sell the contents at public auction, or so much thereof as is required, to pay and discharge the lien and expenses of sale. A notice of the date, time and place of the sale shall be advertised in a newspaper having a general circulation in the county within which the principal office of the safe deposit company, bank, savings bank or savings and loan association is located, at least once a week for two successive weeks prior to the sale. The safe deposit company, bank, savings bank or savings and loan association may retain from the proceeds of sale the amount due to it for its lien and the expenses of sale.

The balance of the proceeds of the sale and the unsold contents, if any, shall be held to be paid and delivered to the lessee or owner of the contents of the vault, safe deposit box or receptacle so sold. If the balance of the proceeds of sale and the unsold contents, if any, remain unclaimed by the owner for the time prescribed in the "Uniform Unclaimed Property Act (1981)," R.S.46:30B-1 et seq., it shall be presumed to be abandoned and disposed of as therein provided.

L.1983, c.566, s.17:14A-51; amended 1989, c.58, s.4.

17:14A-52. Accessibility to vault, safe deposit box or receptacle.

The right of access to a vault, safe deposit box or receptacle rented to a lessee by a safe deposit company shall be governed by the rental agreement, the provisions of P.L.1955, c. 151 (C. 46:39-1 et seq.), R.S. 54:35-19 and R.S. 54:35-20.

L.1983, c. 566, s. 17:14A-52.

17:14A-53. Control of safe deposit company.

It shall be unlawful for any person or company, except with the approval of the commissioner, to acquire control of a safe deposit company incorporated under this chapter.

L.1983, c. 566, s. 17:14A-53.

TITLE 22A. FEES AND COSTS
CHAPTER 2. CIVIL CAUSES
ARTICLE 2. SUPERIOR COURT, LAW DIVISION AND COUNTY CLERK'S OFFICE

22A:2-29. County clerk, deputy clerk of Superior Court, fees.

Upon the filing, indexing, entering or recording of the following documents or papers in the office of the county clerk or deputy clerk of the Superior Court, such parties, filing or having the same recorded or indexed in the county clerk's office or with the deputy clerk of the Superior Court in the various counties in this State in all civil or criminal causes, shall pay the following fees in lieu of the fees heretofore provided for the filing, recording or entering of such documents or papers:

***

Commissions and oaths--

Administering oaths to notaries public and, commissioners of deeds...........................$15.00

For issuing certificate of authority of notary to take proof,
acknowledgment of affidavit...$5.00

For issuing each certificate of the commission and qualification
of notary public for filing with other county clerks..$15.00

For filing each certificate of the commission and qualification
of notary public in office of county clerk of county other than
where such notary has qualified $15.00

***

L. 1953, c. 22, s.11; amended 1957, c. 224; 1965, c. 123, ss. 7,11; 1967, c. 113; 1980, c. 58, s. 2; 1985, c. 422, s. 4; 2001, c. 370, s. 2; 2002, c. 34, s. 31; 2004, c. 108, s. 3.

CHAPTER 4. CERTAIN STATE AND COUNTY OFFICERS

22A:4-14. Acknowledgments, proof, affidavits and oaths.

For a service specified in this section, commissioners of deeds, foreign commissioners of deeds, notaries public, judges and other officers authorized by law to perform such service, shall receive a fee as follows:

For administering an oath or taking an affidavit,...$2.50

For taking proof of a deed, ...$2.50

For taking all acknowledgments,..$2.50

For administering oaths, taking affidavits, taking proofs of a deed, and taking
acknowledgments of the grantors in the transfer of real estate, regardless of
the number of such services performed in a single transaction to transfer
real estate, ...$15.00

For administering oaths, taking affidavits and taking acknowledgments of the
mortgagors in the financing of real estate, regardless of the number of such
services performed in a single transaction to finance real estate, ...$25.00

L. 1953, c. 22, s. 11; amended 1964, c. 205; 2002, c. 34, s. 48.

TITLE 41. OATHS AND AFFIDAVITS

CHAPTER 1. FORMS AND REQUISITES

41:1-7. Seal not necessary to validity of oath or affidavit.

It shall not be necessary to the validity or sufficiency of any oath, affirmation or affidavit, made or taken before any of the persons named in section 41:2-1 of this title, that the same shall be certified under the official seal of the officer before whom made.

CHAPTER 2. ADMINISTERING OATHS; TAKING AFFIDAVITS

41:2-1. Officials authorized to take oaths.

All oaths, affirmations and affidavits required to be made or taken by law of this State, or necessary or proper to be made, taken or used in any court of this State, or for any lawful purpose whatever, may be made and taken before any one of the following officers:

The Chief Justice of the Supreme Court or any of the justices or judges of courts of record of this State;

Masters of the Superior Court;

Municipal judges;

Mayors or aldermen of cities, towns or boroughs or commissioners of commission governed municipalities;

Surrogates, registers of deeds and mortgages, county clerks and their deputies;

Municipal clerks and clerks of boards of chosen freeholders;

Sheriffs of any county;

Members of boards of chosen freeholders;

Clerks of all courts;

Notaries public;

Commissioners of deeds;

Members of the State Legislature;

Attorneys-at-law and counsellors-at-law of this State.

This section shall not apply to official oaths required to be made or taken by any of the officers of this State, nor to oaths or affidavits required to be made and taken in open court.

Amended 1951, c. 302, s. 1; 1953, c. 39, s. 1; 1953, c. 428, s. 3; 1964, c. 165, s. 1; 1968, c. 169; 1970, c. 182; 1983, c. 495; 1986, c. 124; 2007, c. 73.

41:2-3. Oaths administered by notaries public in financial institution matters.

a. A notary public who is a stockholder, director, officer, employee or agent of a financial institution or other corporation may administer an oath to any other stockholder, director, officer, employee or agent of the corporation.

b. A notary public employed by a financial institution may follow directions or policies of the employer which provide that during the hours of the notary public's employment by the financial institution the notary public shall not administer oaths except in the course of the business of the employer.

As used in this section, "financial institution" means a State or federally chartered bank, savings bank, savings and loan association or credit union.

Amended 1997, c. 340.

§ 41:2-14. Oaths of office of notaries, etc.

In case of the absence, removal, death, or any other disability of the county clerk of any county, any judge of the Superior Court may administer the oaths of office and allegiance to commissioners of deeds, notaries public or other persons required to take the same before such clerk, and any official's oath so administered shall be as effectual in law as if taken in the manner prescribed by law.

Amended 1953, c.39, s.10; 1991, c.91, s.407.

41:2-17. Officers authorized to administer or take; jurat; certificate.

Any oath, affirmation or affidavit required or authorized to be taken in any suit or legal proceeding in this state, or for any lawful purpose whatever, except official oaths and depositions required to be taken upon notice, when taken out of this state, may be taken before any notary public of the state, territory, nation, kingdom or country in which the same shall be taken, or before any officer who may be authorized by the laws of this state to take the acknowledgment of deeds in such state, territory, nation, kingdom or country; and a recital that he is such notary or officer in the jurat or certificate of such oath, affirmation or affidavit, and his official designation annexed to his signature, and attested under his official seal, shall be sufficient proof that the person before whom the same is taken is such notary or officer. When, however, any other certificate is required by law to be annexed to the certificate of such officer, other than a notary public, for the recording of a deed acknowledged before him, a like certificate shall be annexed to his certificate of the taking of such oath.

TITLE 46. PROPERTY
SUBTITLE 3. SIGNATURES, SEALS, ACKNOWLEDGMENTS AND PROOFS
CHAPTER 14. ACKNOWLEDGMENTS AND PROOFS

46:14-1. Repealed.

Repealed by L. 1991, c. 308, s. 6, eff. June 1, 1992.

46:14-2. Repealed.

Repealed by L. 1991, c. 308, s. 6, eff. June 1, 1992.

46:14-2.1. Acknowledgment and proof.

a. To acknowledge a deed or other instrument the maker of the instrument shall appear before an officer specified in R.S. 46:14-6.1 and acknowledge that it was executed as the maker's own act. To acknowledge a deed or other instrument made on behalf of a corporation or other entity, the maker shall appear before an officer specified in R.S. 46:14-6.1 and state that the maker was authorized to execute the instrument on behalf of the entity and that the maker executed the instrument as the act of the entity.

b. To prove a deed or other instrument, a subscribing witness shall appear before an officer specified in R.S. 46:14-6.1 and swear that he or she witnessed the maker of the instrument execute the instrument as the maker's own act. To prove a deed or other instrument executed on behalf of a corporation or other entity, a subscribing witness shall appear before an officer specified in R.S. 46:14-6.1 and swear that the representative was authorized to execute the instrument on behalf of the entity, and that he or she witnessed the representative execute the instrument as the act of the entity.

c. The officer taking an acknowledgment or proof shall sign a certificate stating that acknowledgment or proof. The certificate shall also state:

(1) that the maker or the witness personally appeared before the officer;

(2) that the officer was satisfied that the person who made the acknowledgment or proof was the maker of or the witness to the instrument;

(3) the jurisdiction in which the acknowledgment or proof was taken;

(4) the officer's name and title;

(5) the date on which the acknowledgment was taken.

d. The seal of the officer taking the acknowledgment or proof need not be affixed to the certificate stating that acknowledgment or proof.

L. 1991, c. 308, s. 1.

46:14-3. Repealed.

Repealed by L. 1991, c. 308, s. 6, eff. June 1, 1992.

46:14-4. Repealed.

Repealed by L. 1991, c. 308, s. 6, eff. June 1, 1992.

46:14-4.1. Proof of instruments not acknowledged or proved.

If a deed or other instrument cannot be acknowledged or proved for any reason, the instrument may be proved in Superior Court by proof of handwriting or otherwise to the satisfaction of the court. Notice of the application in accordance with the Rules of Court shall be given to any party whose interests may be affected.

L. 1991, c. 308, s. 1.

46:14-4.2. Signatures.

For purposes of this title, a signature includes any mark made on a document by a person who thereby intends to give legal effect to the document. A signature also includes any mark made on a document on behalf of a person, with that person's authority and to effectuate that person's intent.

L. 1991, c. 308, s. 1.

46:14-5. Repealed.

Repealed by L. 1991, c. 308, s. 6, eff. June 1, 1992.

46:14-6. Repealed.

Repealed by L. 1991, c. 308, s. 6, eff. June 1, 1992.

46:14-6.1. Officers authorized to take acknowledgments.

a. The officers of this State authorized to take acknowledgments or proofs in this State, or in any other United States or foreign jurisdiction, are:

(1) an attorney-at-law;

(2) a notary public;

(3) a county clerk or deputy county clerk;

(4) a register of deeds and mortgages or a deputy register;

(5) a surrogate or deputy surrogate.

b. The officers authorized to take acknowledgments or proofs, in addition to those listed in subsection a., are:

(1) any officer of the United States, of a state, territory or district of the United States, or of a foreign nation authorized at the time and place of the acknowledgment or proof by the laws of that jurisdiction to take acknowledgments or proofs. If the certificate of acknowledgment or proof does not designate the officer as a justice, judge or notary, the certificate of acknowledgment or proof, or an affidavit appended to it, shall contain a statement of the officer's authority to take acknowledgments or proofs;

(2) a foreign commissioner of deeds for New Jersey within the jurisdiction of the commission;

(3) a foreign service or consular officer or other representative of the United States to any foreign nation, within the territory of that nation.

L. 1991, c. 308, s. 1.

46:14-7. Repealed.

Repealed by L. 1991, c. 308, s. 6, eff. June 1, 1992.

46:14-8. Repealed.

Repealed by L. 1991, c. 308, s. 6, eff. June 1, 1992.

TITLE 52. STATE GOVERNMENT, DEPARTMENTS AND OFFICERS
SUBTITLE 1. GENERAL PROVISIONS
CHAPTER 7. NOTARIES PUBLIC ACT

§§ 52:7-1 to 52:7-9. Repealed by L. 1979, c. 460, § 11, eff. Feb. 27, 1980.

§ 52:7-10. Short title

This act shall be known and may be cited as the "New Jersey Law on Notarial Acts."

History

L. 1979, c. 460, 1; amended by 2021, c. 179, § 1, effective October 20, 2021.

§ 52:7-10.1. Definitions

As used in P.L.2021, c.179 (C.52:7-10.1 et al.):

a. "Acknowledgment" means a declaration by an individual before a notarial officer that the individual has signed a record for the purpose stated in the record and, if the record is signed in a representative capacity, that the individual signed the record with proper authority and signed it as the act of the individual or entity identified in the record.

b. "Electronic" means relating to technology having electrical, digital, magnetic, wireless, optical, electromagnetic, or similar capabilities.

c. "Electronic signature" means an electronic symbol, sound, or process attached to, or logically associated with, a record and executed or adopted by an individual with the intent to sign the record.

d. "In a representative capacity" means acting as:

(1) An authorized officer, agent, partner, trustee, or other representative for a person other than an individual;

(2) A public officer, personal representative, guardian, or other representative, in the capacity stated in a record;

(3) An agent or attorney-in-fact for a principal; or

(4) An authorized representative of another in any other capacity.

e. "Non-attorney applicant" means an applicant for an initial or renewal commission as a notary public who is not also a licensed attorney-at-law in this State.

f. "Notarial act" means an act, whether performed with respect to a tangible or electronic record, that a notarial officer may perform under the laws of New Jersey. The term includes:

(1) taking an acknowledgment,

(2) administering an oath or affirmation,

(3) taking a verification on oath or affirmation,

(4) witnessing or attesting a signature,

(5) certifying or attesting a copy or deposition, and

(6) noting a protest of a negotiable instrument.

g. "Notarial officer" means a notary public or other individual authorized by law to perform a notarial act.

h. "Notary public" means an individual commissioned by the State Treasurer to perform a notarial act.

i. "Official stamp" means a physical image affixed to or embossed on a tangible record or an electronic image attached to, or logically associated with, an electronic record.

j. "Person" has the meaning ascribed to it in R.S.1:1-2.

k. "Record" means information that is inscribed on a tangible medium or that is stored in an electronic or other medium and is retrievable in perceivable form.

l. "Sign" means, with present intent to authenticate or adopt a record:

(1) To execute or adopt a tangible symbol; or

(2) To attach to or logically associate with the record an electronic symbol, sound, or process.

m. "Signature" means a tangible symbol or an electronic signature that evidences the signing of a record.

n. "Stamping device" means:

(1) A physical device capable of affixing to or embossing on a tangible record an official stamp; or

(2) An electronic device or process capable of attaching to or logically associating with an electronic record an official stamp.

o. "State" means the State of New Jersey; "other state" or "another state" means any state, the District of Columbia, the Commonwealth of Puerto Rico, the United States Virgin Islands, and any other insular possession or territory of the United States other than the State of New Jersey.

p. "Verification on oath or affirmation" means a declaration, made by an individual on oath or affirmation before a notarial officer, that a statement in a record is true.

History

L. 2021, c. 179, § 2, effective October 20, 2021.

§ 52:7-10.2. Course of study; continuing education [Effective July 22, 2022]

a. The provisions of this section do not apply to notaries public who are also licensed attorneys-at-law in this State.

b. A non-attorney applicant for an initial commission as a notary public pursuant to section 2 of P.L.1979, c.460 (C.52:7-11) shall comply with all educational requirements that the State Treasurer shall set forth in rules adopted pursuant to the "Administrative Procedure Act," P.L.1969, c.410 (C.52:14B-1 et seq.). The State Treasurer shall prescribe and approve a course of study to foster and confirm applicants' understanding of the principles and standards that govern notarial practices. Applicants shall be required to acknowledge that they have read and understood the Notary Public Manual and complete any other educational programs that the Treasurer may require.

c. A non-attorney applicant for renewal of a commission pursuant to section 2 of P.L.1979, c.460 (C.52:7-11) who has previously completed the educational requirements required pursuant to subsection b. of this section at least one time, or who was commissioned for the first time before the effective date [Oct. 20, 2021] of P.L.2021, c.179 (C.52:7-10.1 et al.) shall comply with any additional educational requirements that the State Treasurer sets forth in rules adopted pursuant to the "Administrative Procedure Act," P.L.1969, c.410 (C.52:14B-1 et seq.). The State Treasurer shall prescribe and approve a continuing education course for non-attorney applicants seeking a renewal of a commission pursuant to section 2 of P.L.1979, c.460 (C.52:7-11).

d. The State Treasurer shall prescribe an application form and certificate of approval for any notary public course of study and any notary public continuing education course proposed by a provider. The State Treasurer may also provide a notary public course of study and continuing education course.

e. Any course of study developed pursuant to subsections b. and c. of this section may be given by the State Treasurer or by independent vendors.

f. The State Treasurer shall compile a list of all independent vendors offering an approved course of study and continuing education course pursuant to this section and shall provide the list on the website of the State Treasurer.

g. Any course of study for a non-attorney applicant for an initial commission shall cover the statutes, regulations, procedures, and ethics for notaries public as described in the manual issued by the State Treasurer, and shall include the duties and responsibilities of a notary public. The course of study may be provided by classroom instruction, by online instruction, or by any other method approved by the State Treasurer.

h. Any continuing education course for a non-attorney applicant for renewal of a commission shall cover topics which ensure maintenance and enhancement of skill, knowledge, and competency necessary to perform notarial acts. The continuing education course may be provided by online instruction, classroom instruction, or by any other method approved by the State Treasurer.

i. The Treasurer shall regularly assess the efficacy of the State's notarial education program. The Treasurer shall adjust the program's content as notarial technologies and processes evolve, and publish on the Treasury website, on or before September 30 each year, a report on the state of notary education in New Jersey. The report shall contain a summary of commissioning activity, an assessment regarding the need for new or changed educational content, and the estimated timelines for delivering the new or changed content.

History

L. 2021, c. 179, § 6, effective July 22, 2022.

§ 52:7-10.3. Examination [Effective July 22, 2022]

a. The provisions of this section do not apply to applicants who are licensed attorneys-at-law in this State.

b. The State Treasurer shall prescribe an examination to determine the fitness of a non-attorney applicant to exercise the functions of a notary public as provided in section 2 of P.L.1979, c.460 (C.52:7-11). The examination shall:

(1) be based on the statutes, rules, regulations, procedures, and ethical requirements for notaries public as described in the manual issued by the State Treasurer; and

(2) include the requirements, functions, duties, and responsibilities of a notary public.

c. The examination required by subsection b. may be given by the State Treasurer or by an independent vendor under contract to the State Treasurer. If a contract vendor is utilized, the contract vendor shall develop and administer the examination in accordance with specifications approved by the State Treasurer. The State Treasurer shall have the sole responsibility for establishing minimum qualifications and passing requirements of candidates taking the examination.

d. The State Treasurer shall establish a nonrefundable fee which shall be payable at the examination site. Such fee shall be established or changed by the State Treasurer taking into consideration the fee charged by any independent contract vendor to develop and administer the examination, and consideration of the need to defray any proper expenses incurred by the Department of the Treasury in its administration of any independent contract vendor administering the examination. The fee shall not be fixed at a level that will raise amounts in excess of the amount estimated to be so required.

History

L. 2021, c. 179, § 7, effective July 22, 2022.

§ 52:7-10.4. Grounds for State Treasurer to deny application, refuse to renew commission, or revoke, suspend, or limit commission

a. The State Treasurer may deny an application for commission as a notary public; refuse to renew a commission of a notary public; or suspend, revoke, or otherwise limit the commission of a notary public for any act or omission that demonstrates the individual lacks the honesty, integrity, competence, or reliability necessary to act as a notary public, including:

(1) failure to comply with P.L.1979, c.460 (C.52:7-10 et seq.), as amended and supplemented by P.L.2021, c.179 (C.52:7-10.1 et al.);

(2) a fraudulent, dishonest, or deceitful misstatement or omission in the application for commission as a notary public submitted to the State Treasurer;

(3) a finding against, or admission of liability by, the applicant or notary public in any legal proceeding or disciplinary action based on fraud, dishonesty, or deceit, including but not limited to a violation of section 1 of P.L.1997, c.1 (C.2C:21-31) or section 1 of P.L.1994, c.47 (C.2C:21-22), but nothing in this paragraph shall be deemed to supersede P.L.1968, c.282 (C.2A:168A-1 et seq.);

(4) a conviction of a crime of the second degree or above, but nothing in this paragraph shall be deemed to supersede P.L.1968, c.282 (C.2A:168A-1 et seq.);

(5) failure by the notary public to discharge any duty required by any law, including P.L.1979, c.460 (C.52:7-10 et seq.), any rules or regulations promulgated thereunder by the State Treasurer, and any other State or federal law;

(6) use of false or misleading advertising or representation by the notary public representing that the notary is commissioned, licensed, or authorized to practice or engage in work that the notary is not commissioned, licensed, or authorized to engage in;

(7) in the case of a notary public who is not an attorney licensed to practice law, any of the following:

(a) giving legal advice;

(b) acting as an immigration consultant or an expert on immigration matters;

(c) otherwise performing the duties of an attorney licensed to practice law in New Jersey;

(d) a disciplinary or other administrative action resulting in a finding of culpability if the applicant holds any professional license regulated by the State; or

(e) creating or reinforcing, by any means, a false impression that the person is licensed to engage in the practice of law in this State or any other state, including, but not limited to, committing a violation of P.L.1994, c.47 (C.2C:21-22) or P.L.1997, c.1 (C.2C:21-31);

(8) failure to take and subscribe to the oath pursuant to section 5 of P.L.1979, c.460 (C.52:7-14) within three months of the receipt of a notary public commission;

(9) withholding access to or possession of an original record or photocopy provided by a person who seeks performance of a notarial act by the notary public, except where allowed by law; or

(10) the denial of an application for notary public in another state; the refusal to renew in another state; or the suspension, revocation, or other limitation of the commission of the notary public in another state.

b. If the State Treasurer denies an application for notary public; refuses to renew a commission of a notary public; or suspends, revokes, or otherwise limits the commission of a notary public, the applicant or the notary public is entitled to timely notice and hearing in accordance with the "Administrative Procedure Act," P.L.1968, c.410 (C.52:14B-1 et seq.).

c. The authority of the State Treasurer to deny an application for notary public; refuse to renew a commission of a notary public; or suspend, revoke, or otherwise limit the commission of a notary public shall not prevent a person aggrieved by the actions of a notary public from seeking other criminal or civil remedies provided by law.

History

L. 2021, c. 179, § 9, effective October 20, 2021.

§ 52:7-10.5. Official stamp

a. The official stamp of a notary public shall:

(1) include the name of the notary public, the title "Notary Public, State of New Jersey," and the notary public's commission expiration date; and

(2) be capable of being copied together with the record to which it is affixed or attached or with which it is logically associated.

b. If a notarial act regarding a tangible record is performed by a notary public, an official stamp shall be affixed to or embossed on the certificate near the signature of the notary public so as to be clear and readable. If a notarial act regarding an electronic record is performed by a notary public and the certificate contains the information specified in subsection a. of this section, an official stamp must be attached to or logically associated with the certificate.

History

L. 2021, c. 179, § 14, effective October 20, 2021.

§ 52:7-10.6. Stamping device

a. A notary public is responsible for the security of the stamping device used by the notary public and may not allow another individual to use the device to perform a notarial act, except at the specific instruction of a notary public who cannot physically use the stamping device.

b. The stamping device is the property of the notary public and not of the notary public's employer, even if the employer paid for the stamping device.

c. If the stamping device used by the notary public is lost or stolen, the notary public or the notary public's personal representative shall notify the State Treasurer of the loss or theft within 10 days.

History

L. 2021, c. 179, § 15, effective October 20, 2021.

§ 52:7-10.7. Authority to perform notarial act

a. A notarial officer may perform a notarial act authorized by P.L.1979, c.460 (C.52:7-10 et seq.), as amended and supplemented by P.L.2021, c.179 (C.52:7-10.1 et al.), and any other applicable law.

b. A notarial officer may not perform a notarial act with respect to a record to which the officer or the officer's spouse or civil union partner is a party, or in which either of them has a direct beneficial interest. A notarial act performed in violation of this subsection is voidable.

c. A notarial officer may certify that a tangible copy of an electronic record is an accurate copy of the electronic record.

History

L. 2021, c. 179, § 16, effective October 20, 2021.

§ 52:7-10.8. Requirements for certain notarial acts

a. A notarial officer who takes an acknowledgment of a record shall determine, from personal knowledge or satisfactory evidence of the identity of the individual, that the individual appearing before the officer and making the acknowledgment has the identity claimed and that the signature on the record is the signature of the individual.

b. A notarial officer who takes a verification of a statement on oath or affirmation shall determine, from personal knowledge or satisfactory evidence of the identity of the individual, that the individual appearing before the officer and making the verification has the identity claimed and that the signature on the statement verified is the signature of the individual.

c. A notarial officer who witnesses or attests to a signature shall determine, from personal knowledge or satisfactory evidence of the identity of the individual, that the individual appearing before the officer and signing the record has the identity claimed.

d. A notarial officer who certifies or attests a copy of a record or an item that was copied shall determine that the copy is a full, true, and accurate transcription or reproduction of the record or item.

e. A notarial officer who makes or notes a protest of a negotiable instrument shall determine the matters set forth in subsection b. of N.J.S.12A:3-505.

f. For the purposes of this section:

(1) A notarial officer has personal knowledge of the identity of an individual appearing before the notarial officer if the individual is personally known to the notarial officer through dealings sufficient to provide reasonable certainty that the individual has the identity claimed.

(2) A notarial officer has satisfactory evidence of the identity of an individual appearing before the notarial officer if the notarial officer can identify the individual by means of:

(a) A passport, driver's license, or government-issued, non-driver identification card, which is current or expired not more than three years before the performance of the notarial act; or

(b) Another form of government-issued identification, which is current or expired not more than three years before the performance of the notarial act, and which:

(i) contains the individual's signature or a photograph of the individual's face; and

(ii) is satisfactory to the notarial officer; or

(c) A verification of oath or affirmation of a credible witness personally appearing before the notarial officer or using communication technology to appear before the notarial officer pursuant to section 19 of P.L.2021, c.179 (C.52:7-10.10) and personally known to the notarial officer or whom the notarial officer can identify on the basis of a passport, driver's license, or government-issued, non-driver identification card, which is current or expired not more than three years before the performance of the notarial act.

(3) A notarial officer may require an individual to provide additional information or identification credentials necessary to assure the notarial officer of the identity of the individual.

History

L. 2021, c. 179, § 17, effective October 20, 2021.

§ 52:7-10.9. Personal appearance; use of communication technology

If a notarial act relates to a statement made in, or a signature executed on, a record, the individual making the statement or executing the signature shall appear personally before the notarial officer or shall use communication technology to appear before the notarial officer pursuant to section 19 of P.L.2021, c.179 (C.52:7-10.10).

History

L. 2021, c. 179, § 18, effective October 20, 2021.

§ 52:7-10.10. Notarial act performed by remotely located individual

a. As used in this section:

(1) "Communication technology" means an electronic device or process that:

(a) allows a notarial officer and a remotely located individual to communicate with each other simultaneously by sight and sound; and

(b) when necessary and consistent with other applicable law, facilitates communication with a remotely located individual who has a vision, hearing, or speech impairment.

(2) "Foreign state" means a jurisdiction other than the United States, a state, or a federally recognized Indian tribe.

(3) "Identity proofing" means a process or service by which a third person provides a notarial officer with a means to verify the identity of a remotely located individual by a review of personal information from public or private data sources.

(4) "Outside the United States" means a location outside the geographic boundaries of the United States, Puerto Rico, the United States Virgin Islands, and any territory, insular possession, or other location subject to the jurisdiction of the United States.

(5) "Remotely located individual" means an individual who is not in the physical presence of a notarial officer performing a notarial act under subsection c.

b. This section does not apply to a record to the extent it is governed by a law governing the creation and execution of wills or codicils, except that subsections e., f., g., and h. of this section shall apply to notarial acts performed on a tangible record that is governed by a law governing the creation or execution of wills and codicils.

c. A remotely located individual may comply with section 18 of P.L.2021, c.179 (C.52:7-10.9) and subsections a. and b. of R.S.46:14-2.1 by using communication technology to appear before a notarial officer.

d. A notarial officer located in this State may perform a notarial act using communication technology for a remotely located individual if:

(1) the notarial officer:

(a) has personal knowledge pursuant to paragraph (1) of subsection f. of section 17 of P.L.2021, c.179 (C.52:7-10.8) of the identity of the individual;

(b) has satisfactory evidence of the identity of the remotely located individual by oath or affirmation from a credible witness appearing before the notarial officer pursuant to paragraph (2) of subsection f. of section 17 of P.L.2021, c.179 (C.52:7-10.8.) or using communication technology to appear before the notarial officer pursuant to this section; or

(c) has obtained satisfactory evidence of the identity of the remotely located individual by using at least two different types of identity proofing;

(2) the notarial officer is able reasonably to confirm that a record before the notarial officer is the same record in which the remotely located individual made a statement or on which the remotely located individual executed a signature;

(3) the notarial officer, or a person acting on behalf of the notarial officer, creates an audio-visual recording of the performance of the notarial act; and

(4) for a remotely located individual who is located outside the United States:

(a) the record:

(i) is to be filed with or relates to a matter before a public official or court, governmental entity, or other entity subject to the jurisdiction of the United States; or

(ii) involves property located in the territorial jurisdiction of the United States or involves a transaction substantially connected with the United States; and

(b) the act of making the statement or signing the record is not prohibited by the foreign state in which the remotely located individual is located.

e. A notarial officer in this State may use communication technology under subsection d. of this section to take an acknowledgement of a signature on a tangible record that is in the possession of the notary public if the record is displayed to and identified by the remotely located individual during the audio-visual session required by paragraph (3) of subsection d. of this section.

f. A notarial officer's obligation under paragraph (2) of subsection d. of this section for the performance of a notarial act with respect to a tangible record not physically present before the notarial officer is satisfied if:

(1) the remotely located individual:

(a) during the audio-visual session required by paragraph (3) of subsection d. of this section, signs:

(i) the record; and

(ii) a declaration, substantially in the following form, which is part of or securely attached to the record:

> I declare under penalty of perjury that the record to which this declaration is attached is the same record on which performed a notarial act and before whom I appeared by means of communication technology on [date].
>
> _____ Printed name of remotely located individual
> _____ Signature of remotely located individual; and

(b) sends the record and declaration to the notarial officer not later than three days after the notarial act was performed; and

(2) the notarial officer:

(a) in the audio-visual recording required by paragraph (3) of subsection d. of this section, records the individual signing the record and declaration; and

(b) after receipt of the record and declaration from the individual, executes the certificate of notarial act required by section 13 of P.L.2021, c.179 (C.52:7-10.19), which must include the following statement or words of similar import:

> "I [name of notarial officer] witnessed, by means of communication technology, [name of remotely located individual] sign the attached record and declaration on [date]".

g. A notarial act performed in compliance with subsection f. of this section complies with paragraph (1) of subsection a. of section 13 of P.L.2021, c.179 (C.52:7-10.19) and is effective as of the date on which the declaration was signed by the remotely located individual.

h. Subsections f. and g. of this section are not intended to exclude other procedures to satisfy the requirements of this section for a notarial act performed with respect to a tangible record.

i. A notarial officer in this State may administer an oath to a remotely located individual using communication technology. Except as required or permitted by rule or law of this State, the notarial officer shall identify the individual under paragraph (1) of subsection d. of this section, create an audio-visual recording under paragraph (3) of subsection d. of this section of the individual taking the oath, and preserve a copy of the audio-visual recording under subsection l. of this section.

j. If a notarial act is performed under this section, the certificate of notarial act required by section 10 of P.L.1979, c.460 (C.52:7-19), the certificate required by section c. of R.S.46:14-2.1, or the short-form certificate provided in section 21 of P.L.2021, c.179 (C.52:7-10.12) must indicate that the notarial act was performed using communication technology.

k. A short-form certificate provided in section 21 of P.L.2021, c.179 (C.52:7-10.12) for a notarial act subject to this section is sufficient if it:

(1) complies with any rules or regulations adopted by the State Treasurer under paragraph (1) of subsection o. of this section or section 29 of P.L.2021, c.179 (C.52:7-10.20); or

(2) is in the form provided by section 21 of P.L.2021, c.179 (C.52:7-10.12) and contains a statement substantially as follows: "This notarial act involved the use of communication technology."

l. A notarial officer, a guardian, conservator, or agent of a notarial officer, or a personal representative of a deceased notarial officer, shall retain the audio-visual recording created under paragraph (3) of subsection d. of this section or cause the recording to be retained by a repository designated by or on behalf of the person required to retain the recording. Unless a different period is required by any rule or regulation adopted by the State Treasurer under paragraph (4) of subsection o. of this section, the recording must be retained for a period of at least 10 years after the recording is made.

m. Before a notary public performs the notary public's initial notarial act under this section, the notary public must notify the State Treasurer that the notary public will be performing such notarial acts and identify the technologies the notary public intends to use.

n. If the State Treasurer has established standards under subsection i. of this section and section 29 of P.L.2021, c.179 (C.52:7-10.20) for approval of communication technology or identity proofing, the communication technology and identity proofing must conform to those standards.

o. In addition to adopting rules and regulations pursuant to the "Administrative Procedure Act," P.L.1968, c.410 (C.52:14B-1 et seq.) under section 29 of P.L.2021,

c.179 (C.52:7-10.20), the State Treasurer may adopt rules and regulations pursuant to the "Administrative Procedure Act," P.L.1968, c.410 (C.52:14B-1 et seq.) under this section regarding the performance of a notarial act. The rules and regulations may:

(1) prescribe the means of performing a notarial act involving a remotely located individual using communication technology;

(2) establish standards for communication technology and identity proofing;

(3) establish requirements or procedures to approve providers of communication technology and the process of identity proofing;

(4) establish standards and a period for the retention of an audio-visual recording created under paragraph (3) of subsection d. of this section; and

(5) prescribe methods for confirmation of a tangible record by a notarial officer permitted under subsection e. of this section.

p. Before adopting, amending, or repealing a rule or regulation governing performance of a notarial act with respect to a remotely located individual, the State Treasurer must consider:

(1) the most recent standards regarding the performance of a notarial act with respect to a remotely located individual promulgated by national standard-setting organizations such as the Mortgage Industry Standards Maintenance Organization and the recommendations of the National Association of Secretaries of State;

(2) standards, practices, and customs of other jurisdictions that have laws substantially similar to this section; and

(3) the views of governmental officials and entities and other interested persons.

q. (1) A notarial officer may perform a notarial act using communication technology for a remotely located individual that meets the requirements of section 19 of P.L.2021, c.179 (C.52:7-10.10) and subsections a. and b. of R.S.46:14-2.1 regardless of whether the remotely located individual is physically located in this State.

(2) A notarial act performed using communication technology for a remotely located individual is deemed performed in New Jersey and is governed by New Jersey law.

It is the intent of the Legislature that, to the fullest extent allowed by the Full Faith and Credit Clause of the United States Constitution and the laws of the 50 states and the District of Columbia, a notarial act performed in this State shall be recognized, be enforceable, and have the same effect under the law of the 50 states as if performed by a notarial officer of those jurisdictions.

s. By allowing its communication technology or identity proofing to facilitate a notarial act for a remotely located individual or by providing storage of the audio-visual recording created under paragraph (3) of subsection d. of this section, the provider of the communication technology, identity proofing, or storage appoints the State Treasurer as the provider's agent for service of process in any civil action in this State related to the notarial act.

History

L. 2021, c. 179, § 19, effective October 20, 2021.

§ 52:7-10.11. Signature if individual unable to sign

If an individual is physically unable to sign a record, the individual may direct an individual other than the notarial officer to sign the record with the individual's name.

The notarial officer shall insert "Signature affixed by (name of other individual) at the direction of (name of individual)" or words of similar import.

History

L. 2021, c. 179, § 20, effective October 20, 2021.

§ 52:7-10.12. Certificate form

The following short form certificates of notarial acts are sufficient for the purposes indicated, if the requirements of section 10 of P.L.1979, c.460 (C.52:7-19) are satisfied.

Certificates of notarial acts are deemed sufficient for the purposes indicated if substantially all of the requirements of section 10 of P.L.1979, c.460 (C.52:7-19) and this section are satisfied:

a. For an acknowledgment in an individual capacity:

State of _____
County of _____

This record was acknowledged before me on _____ (date) by (Name(s) of individual(s)).

Signature of notarial officer
Stamp
Title of office
(My commission expires: _____)

b. For an acknowledgment in a representative capacity:

State of _____
County of _____

This record was acknowledged before me on _____ (date) by (Name(s) of individual(s)) as (type of authority, such as officer or trustee) of (name of party on behalf of whom record was executed)..

Signature of notarial officer
Stamp
Title of office
(My commission expires: _____)

c. For a verification on oath or affirmation:

State of _____
County of _____

Signed and sworn to (or affirmed) before me on _____ (date) by (Name(s) of individual(s) making statement).

Signature of notarial officer
Stamp
Title of office
(My commission expires: _____)

d. For witnessing or attesting a signature:

State of _____
County of _____

Signed (or attested) before me on _____ (date) by (Name(s) of individual(s)).

Signature of notarial officer
Stamp
Title of office
(My commission expires: _____)

e. For certifying a copy of a record:

State of _____
County of _____

I certify that this is a true and correct copy of a record in the possession of
_____ (name).
Dated _____

Signature of notarial officer
Stamp
Title of office
(My commission expires: _____)

History

L. 2021, c. 179, § 21, effective October 20, 2021.

§ 52:7-10.13. Notarial act in this State

a. The signature and title of an individual performing a notarial act are prima facie evidence that the signature is genuine and that the individual holds the designated title.

b. A notarial act may be performed in this State by an individual authorized by the applicable law to perform the notarial act.

c. The signature and title of a notarial officer authorized by the applicable law to perform the notarial act conclusively establishes the authority of the officer to perform the notarial act.

History

L. 2021, c. 179, § 22, effective October 20, 2021.

§ 52:7-10.14. Notarial acts outside this state

a. In Another State.

(1) A notarial act performed in another state has the same effect under the law of this State as if performed by a notarial officer of this State, if the act performed in that state is performed by:

(a) a notary public of that state;

(b) a judge, clerk, or deputy clerk of a court of that state; or

(c) any other individual authorized by the law of that state to perform the notarial act.

(2) The signature and title of an individual performing a notarial act in another state are prima facie evidence that the signature is genuine and that the individual holds the designated title.

(3) The signature and title of a notarial officer described in subparagraph (a) or (b) of paragraph (1) of this subsection conclusively establish the authority of the officer to perform the notarial act.

b. Under Authority of Federally Recognized Indian Tribe.

(1) A notarial act performed under the authority and in the jurisdiction of a federally recognized Indian tribe has the same effect as if performed by a notarial officer of this State, if the act performed in the jurisdiction of the tribe is performed by:

(a) a notary public of the tribe;

(b) a judge, clerk, or deputy clerk of a court of the tribe; or

(c) any other individual authorized by the law of the tribe to perform the notarial act.

(2) The signature and title of an individual performing a notarial act under the authority of and in the jurisdiction of a federally recognized Indian tribe are prima facie evidence that the signature is genuine and that the individual holds the designated title.

(3) The signature and title of a notarial officer described in subparagraph (a) or (b) of paragraph (1) of this subsection conclusively establish the authority of the officer to perform the notarial act.

c. Under Federal Authority.

(1) A notarial act performed under federal law has the same effect under the law of this State as if performed by a notarial officer of this State, if the act performed under federal law is performed by:

(a) a judge, clerk, or deputy clerk of a court;

(b) an individual in military service or performing duties under the authority of military service who is authorized to perform notarial acts under federal law;

(c) an individual designated a notarizing officer by the United States Department of State for performing notarial acts overseas; or

(d) any other individual authorized by federal law to perform the notarial act.

(2) The signature and title of an individual acting under federal authority and performing a notarial act are prima facie evidence that the signature is genuine and that the individual holds the designated title.

(3) The signature and title of an officer described in subparagraph (a), (b), or (c) of paragraph (1) of this subsection conclusively establish the authority of the officer to perform the notarial act.

d. Foreign Notarial Acts.

(1) As used in this subsection, "foreign state" means a jurisdiction other than the United States, a state, or a federally recognized Indian tribe.

(2) If a notarial act is performed under authority and in the jurisdiction of a foreign state or constituent unit of the foreign state or is performed under the authority of a multinational or international governmental organization, the act has the same effect under the law of this State as if performed by a notarial officer of this State.

(3) If the title of office and indication of authority to perform notarial acts in a foreign state appears in a digest of foreign law or in a list customarily used as a source for that information, the authority of an officer with that title to perform notarial acts is conclusively established.

(4) The signature and official stamp of an individual holding an office described in paragraph (3) of this subsection are prima facie evidence that the signature is genuine and the individual holds the designated title.

(5) An apostille in the form prescribed by the Hague Convention of October 5, 1961 and issued by a foreign state party to the Hague Convention conclusively establishes that the signature of the notarial officer is genuine and that the notarial officer holds the indicated office.

(6) A consular authentication issued by an individual designated by the United States Department of State as a notarizing officer for performing notarial acts overseas and

attached to the record with respect to which the notarial act is performed conclusively establishes that the signature of the notarial officer is genuine and that the notarial officer holds the indicated office.

History

L. 2021, c. 179, § 23, effective October 20, 2021.

§ 52:7-10.15. Notification regarding performance of notarial act on electronic record; selection of technology; acceptance of tangible copy of electronic record

a. A notarial officer may select one or more tamper-evident technologies to perform notarial acts with respect to electronic records. A person may not require a notarial officer to perform a notarial act with respect to an electronic record with a technology that the notarial officer has not selected.

b. Before a notary public performs the notary public's initial notarial act with respect to an electronic record, the notary public shall notify the State Treasurer that the notary public will be performing notarial acts with respect to electronic records and identify the technology that the notary public intends to use. If the State Treasurer has established standards for approval of technology pursuant to section 29 of P.L.2021, c.179 (C.52:7-10.20), the technology must conform to those standards. If the technology conforms to the standards, the State Treasurer shall approve the use of the technology.

c. A county clerk, a register of deeds and mortgages, and a county surrogate shall accept for recording a tangible copy of an electronic record containing a notarial certificate as satisfying any requirement that a record accepted for recording be an original, if the notarial officer executing the notarial certificate certifies that the tangible copy is an accurate copy of the electronic record.

History

L. 2021, c. 179, § 24, effective October 20, 2021.

§ 52:7-10.16. Database of notaries public

The State Treasurer shall maintain an electronic database of current and former notaries public, including the dates that the notary public was commissioned and authorized to perform notarial acts:

a. through which a person may verify the authority of a notary public to perform notarial acts; and

b. which indicates whether a notary public has notified the State Treasurer that the notary public will be performing notarial acts on electronic records.

History

L. 2021, c. 179, § 25, effective October 20, 2021.

§ 52:7-10.17. Authority to refuse to perform notarial act

a. A notarial officer may refuse to perform a notarial act if the officer is not satisfied that:

(1) the individual executing the record is competent or has the capacity to execute the record;

(2) the individual's signature is knowingly and voluntarily made;

(3) the individual's signature on the record or statement substantially conforms to the signature on a form of identification used to determine the identity of the individual; or

(4) the physical appearance of the individual signing the record or statement substantially conforms to the photograph on a form of identification used to determine the identity of the individual.

b. A notarial officer may refuse to perform a notarial act unless refusal is prohibited by law other than P.L.1979, c.460 (C.52:7-10 et seq.), as amended and supplemented by P.L.2021, c.179 (C.52:7-10.1 et al.).

History

L. 2021, c. 179, § 26, effective October 20, 2021.

§ 52:7-10.18. Journal

a. A notary public shall maintain a journal of all notarial acts performed.

(1) The journal may be created and maintained on a tangible medium or in an electronic format.

(2) A notary public shall maintain only one journal at a time to chronicle all notarial acts, whether those notarial acts are performed regarding tangible or electronic records.

(3) If the journal is maintained on a tangible medium, it shall be a permanent, bound register with consecutively numbered lines and consecutively numbered pages.

(4) If the journal is maintained in an electronic format, it shall be in a permanent, tamper-evident electronic format complying with any rules and regulations promulgated by the State Treasurer.

b. For each notarial act, the notary public shall record in the journal:

(1) the date and time of the notarial act;

(2) the type of notarial act, including but not limited to the taking of an acknowledgment, the taking of a proof of a deed, the administration of an oath, or the taking of an affidavit;

(3) the name and address of each person for whom the notarial act is performed;

(4) if the identity of the individual is based on personal knowledge, a statement to that effect;

(5) if the identity of the individual is based on satisfactory evidence, a brief description of the method of identification and the identification credential presented, if any, including, if applicable, the type, date of issuance, and date of expiration of an identification document, or the name and signature of any identifying witness and, if applicable, the type, date of issuance, and date of expiration of a document identifying the witness; and

(6) an itemized list of all fees charged for the notarial act.

c. If a notary public's journal is lost or stolen, the notary public shall notify the State Treasurer within 10 days of the loss or theft.

d. The notary public shall either:

(1) retain the journal for 10 years after the performance of the last notarial act chronicled in the journal; or

(2) transmit the journal to the Department of the Treasury, Division of Revenue and Enterprise Services, or a repository approved by the State Treasurer.

e. On resignation from, or the revocation or suspension of, a notary public's commission, the notary public shall either:

(1) retain the journal in accordance with paragraph (1) of subsection d. of this section and inform the State Treasurer where the journal is located; or

(2) transmit the journal to the Department of the Treasury, Division of Revenue and Enterprise Services, or a repository approved by the State Treasurer.

f. On the death or adjudication of incompetency of a current or former notary public, the notary public's personal representative or guardian or any other person knowingly in possession of the journal shall, within 45 days, transmit it to the Department of the Treasury, Division of Revenue and Enterprise Services, or a repository approved by the State Treasurer.

g. In lieu of maintaining a journal, a notary public who is an attorney-at-law admitted to practice in this State, or who is employed by an attorney-at-law, or who is employed by or acting as an agent for a title insurance company licensed to do business in this State pursuant to P.L.2001, c.210 (C.17:22A-26 et seq.), may maintain a record of notarial acts in the form of files regularly maintained for the attorney's law practice or the title insurance company's business activities, as the case may be.

History

L. 2021, c. 179, § 27, effective October 20, 2021.

§ 52:7-10.19. Validity of notarial acts

a. Except as otherwise provided in section 9 of P.L.2021, c.179 (C.52:7-10.4), the failure of a notarial officer to perform a duty or meet a requirement specified in P.L.1979, c.460 (C.52:7-10 et seq.), as amended and supplemented by P.L.2021, c.179 (C.52:7-10.1 et al.), does not invalidate a notarial act performed by the notarial officer.

b. The validity of a notarial act under P.L.1979, c.460 (C.52:7-10 et seq.), as amended and supplemented by P.L.2021, c.179 (C.52:7-10.1 et al.), does not prevent an aggrieved person from seeking to invalidate the record or transaction that is the subject of the notarial act or from seeking other remedies available by law and as provided in P.L.1979, c.460 (C.52:7-10 et seq.), as amended and supplemented by P.L.2021, c.179 (C.52:7-10.1 et al.).

c. P.L.1979, c.460 (C.52:7-10 et seq.), as amended and supplemented by P.L.2021, c.179 (C.52:7-10.1 et al.), shall not validate any purported notarial act performed by an individual who does not have the authority to perform notarial acts.

History

L. 2021, c. 179, § 28, effective October 20, 2021.

§ 52:7-10.20. Rules and regulations

a. The State Treasurer shall adopt rules and regulations pursuant to the "Administrative Procedure Act," P.L.1968, c.410 (C.52:14B-1 et seq.) to implement the provisions of P.L.1979, c.460 (C.52:7-10 et seq.), as amended and supplemented by P.L.2021, c.179 (C.52:7-10.1 et al.). Any rules and regulations regarding the performance of notarial acts with respect to electronic records shall not require, or accord greater legal status or effect to, the implementation or application of a specific technology or technical specification. The rules and regulations may:

(1) prescribe the manner of performing notarial acts regarding tangible and electronic records;

(2) include provisions to ensure that any change to or tampering with a record bearing a certificate of a notarial act is self-evident;

(3) include provisions to ensure integrity in the creation, transmittal, storage, or authentication of electronic records or signatures;

(4) prescribe the process of granting, renewing, conditioning, denying, suspending, revoking, or otherwise limiting a notary public commission and assuring the trustworthiness of an individual holding a commission as notary public;

(5) include provisions to prevent fraud or mistake in the performance of notarial acts; and

(6) provide for the administration of the examination under section 7 of P.L.2021, c.179 (C.52:7-10.3) and the course of study under section 6 of P.L.2021, c.179 (C.52:7-10.2).

b. In adopting, amending, or repealing rules and regulations concerning notarial acts with respect to electronic records, the State Treasurer shall consider, consistent with the provisions of P.L.1979, c.460 (C.52:7-10 et seq.), as amended and supplemented by P.L.2021, c.179 (C.52:7-10.1 et al.):

(1) the most recent standards regarding electronic records promulgated by national bodies, such as the Mortgage Industry Standards Maintenance Organization and the National Association of Secretaries of State;

(2) standards, practices, and customs of other jurisdictions that substantially enact the Revised Uniform Law on Notarial Acts, as embodied in P.L.1979, c.460 (C.52:7-10 et seq.), as amended and supplemented by P.L.2021, c.179 (C.52:7-10.1 et al.); and

(3) the views of governmental officials and entities and other interested persons.

History

L. 2021, c. 179, § 29, effective October 20, 2021.

§ 52:7-10.21. Relation to electronic signatures in global and national commerce act

P.L.2021, c.179 (C.52:7-10.1 et al.) modifies, limits, and supersedes the Electronic Signatures in Global and National Commerce Act, 15 U.S.C. § 7001 et seq., but does not modify, limit, or supersede section 101(c) of that act, 15 U.S.C. § 7001(c), or authorize electronic delivery of any of the notices described in section 103(b) of that act, 15 U.S.C. § 7003(b).

History

L. 2021, c. 179, § 34, effective October 20, 2021.

§ 52:7-10.22. Savings clause

P.L.1979, c.460 (C.52:7-10 et seq.), as amended and supplemented by P.L.2021, c.179 (C.52:7-10.1 et al.), shall not affect the validity or effect of any notarial act performed before the effective date [Oct. 20, 2021] of P.L.2021, c.179 (C.52:7-10.1 et al.).

History

L. 2021, c. 179, § 35, effective October 20, 2021.

§ 52:7-10.23. Rules, regulations

Notwithstanding the provisions of the "Administrative Procedure Act," P.L.1968, c.410 (C.52:14B-1 et seq.) to the contrary, the State Treasurer shall adopt, after notice, interim rules and regulations as shall be necessary for the implementation of this act [C.52:7-10.1 et al.] within 90 days after the effective date of this act. The rules and regulations shall be effective as regulations immediately upon filing with the Office of Administrative Law and shall be effective for a period not to exceed 18 months, and may, thereafter, be amended, adopted or readopted by the Treasurer in accordance with the provisions of the "Administrative Procedure Act," P.L.1968, c.410 (C.52:14B-1 et seq.).

History

L. 2021, c. 179, § 38, effective October 20, 2021.

§ 52:7-11. Commission; term; application; renewal

a. The State Treasurer may commission so many notaries public as the State Treasurer deems necessary to commission. Notaries public shall hold their respective offices for a term of five years.

b. An applicant for commission as a notary public shall make application to the State Treasurer on a form prescribed by the State Treasurer and endorsed by a member of the Legislature. Renewals shall be made in the same manner as the original application. All applications shall be submitted electronically.

The application form shall provide a notice to the applicant that a notary public who is not licensed as an attorney-at-law shall not use or advertise the title of lawyer or attorney-at-law, or equivalent terms, in any language, which mean or imply that the notary public is licensed as an attorney-at-law in the State of New Jersey or in any other jurisdiction of the United States. The application form shall also state that a notary public who advertises the notary public's services in any language is required to provide with such advertisement a notice in the language of the advertisement which contains the following statement or translation of the following statement if the advertisement is not in English: "I am not an attorney licensed to practice law and may not give legal advice about immigration or any other legal matter or accept fees for legal advice."

c. The State Treasurer shall collect a nonrefundable fee of $25 for each commission or renewal. In collecting the fee, the State Treasurer shall accept the use of a credit card, debit card, or electronic funds transfer.

History

L. 1979, c. 460, § 2; amended 1987, c. 435, § 21; 2014, c. 48, § 3, eff. Dec. 9, 2014; 2021, c. 179, § 3, effective October 20, 2021.

§ 52:7-12. Qualifications

a. A person commissioned as a notary public in this State shall:

(1) be at the time of appointment at least 18 years of age;

(2) be at the time of appointment a legal resident of this State or have a place of employment or practice in this State; and

(3) not be disqualified to receive a commission under section 9 of P.L.2021, c.179 (C.52:7-10.4 et al.).

b. A non-attorney applicant for an initial commission as a notary public shall provide satisfactory proof that the applicant has:

(1) completed a course of study approved by the State Treasurer pursuant to subsection b. of section 6 of P.L.2021, c.179 (C.52:7-10.2); and

(2) passed an examination prescribed by the State Treasurer pursuant to section 7 of P.L.2021, c.179 (C.52:7-10.3).

c. A non-attorney commissioned notary public applying to renew a commission who has satisfactorily completed a course of study required pursuant to subsection b. of section 6 of P.L.2021, c.179 (C.52:7-10.2) at least one time, or who was commissioned for the first time before the effective date of P.L.2021, c.179 (C.52:7-10.1 et al.) shall complete a continuing education course as set forth in subsection c. of section 6 of P.L.2021, c.179 (C.52:7-10.2) and provide satisfactory proof of such completion.

History

L. 1979, c. 460, 3; amended by 2021, c. 179, § 4, effective October 20, 2021.

§ 52:7-13. Commission of nonresidents; additional requirements

a. No person shall be denied a commission as a notary public on account of residence outside this State, provided such person maintains, or is regularly employed in, an office in this State or is an employee of a business with its domicile or primary place of business in this State and performs his employment duties remotely from a home office or a co-working space.

b. In addition to the requirements of section 3 of P.L.1979, c.460 (C.52:7-12), any non-resident shall file with the State Treasurer at the time of application a certificate setting forth the residence and the address of the applicant, and the office or place of employment of the applicant in this State.

c. Once commissioned, any such nonresident notary public shall file with the State Treasurer a certificate showing any change of residence or change of the office or place of employment of the notary public in this State.

History

L. 1979, c. 460, § 4; amended 2014, c. 48, § 4, eff. Dec. 9, 2014; 2021, c. 179, § 5, effective October 20, 2021.

§ 52:7-14. Oath; filing; certificate of commission

a. Within three months of the receipt of a commission, each notary public shall take and subscribe an oath before the clerk of the county in which the notary public resides, to faithfully and honestly discharge the duties of the office; and make and keep a true record of all such matters as are required by law, which oath shall be filed with the clerk. The oath of office of a nonresident notary public shall be taken and subscribed before the clerk of the county in which the nonresident notary public maintains the notary public's office or the county in which the nonresident notary public is an employee of a business with its domicile or primary place of business in this State.

b. Upon the administration of the oath, the clerk shall cause the notary public to endorse the certificate of commission and qualification and shall transmit the certificate to the State Treasurer within 10 days of the administration of the oath. After the administration of the oath, the clerk shall provide a notice to the person that a notary public who is not licensed as an attorney-at-law shall not use or advertise the title of lawyer or attorney-at-law, or equivalent terms, in any language, which mean or imply that the notary public is licensed as an attorney-at-law in the State of New Jersey or in any other jurisdiction of the United States. The notice shall also state that a notary public who advertises the notary public's services, in any language, is required to provide with such advertisement a notice in the language of the advertisement which contains the following statement or translation of the following statement if the advertisement is not in English:

> "I am not an attorney licensed to practice law and may not give legal advice about immigration or any other legal matter or accept fees for legal advice."

c. The State Treasurer shall cancel and revoke the appointment of any notary public who fails to take and subscribe the oath within three months of the receipt of the commission and any appointment so canceled and revoked shall be null, void and of no effect. A commission authorizes the notary public to perform notarial acts. The commission does not provide the notary public any immunity or benefit conferred by the law of this State on public officials or employees.

History

L. 1979, c. 460, § 5; amended 2014, c. 48, § 5, eff. Dec. 9, 2014; 2021, c. 179, § 8, effective October 20, 2021.

§ 52:7-15. Statewide authority

A notary public who has been duly commissioned and qualified is authorized to perform the duties of a notary public throughout the State.

History

L. 1979, c. 460, 6; amended by 2021, c. 179, § 10, effective October 20, 2021.

§ 52:7-16. Repealed by L. 2021, c. 179, § 37, effective October 20, 2021.

§ 52:7-17. Manual

a. The State Treasurer shall maintain a manual on the Department of the Treasury's website that sets forth the requirements, functions, duties, and responsibilities of a notary public. The manual shall include, but not be limited to, the statutes, rules, regulations, procedures, and ethical requirements governing a notary public.

b. The manual shall specify that a notary public who is not licensed as an attorney-at-law shall not use or advertise the title of lawyer or attorney-at-law, or equivalent terms, in any language, which mean or imply that the notary public is licensed as an attorney-atlaw in the State of New Jersey or in any other jurisdiction of the United States. The manual shall also state that a notary public who advertises the notary public's services in any language is required to provide with such advertisement a notice which contains the following statement or translation of the following statement if the advertisement is not in English: "I am not an attorney licensed to practice law and may not give legal advice about immigration or any other legal matter or accept fees for legal advice." The manual shall also state that no person shall be commissioned a notary public or receive a renewal of a notary public commission if that person has been convicted under the laws of this State of an offense involving dishonesty, including but not limited to a violation of section 1 of P.L.1997, c.1 (C.2C:21-31) or section 1 of P.L.1994, c.47 (C.2C:21-22), or a substantially similar crime under the laws of another state or the United States or of a crime of the second degree or above, but nothing in this paragraph shall be deemed to supersede P.L.1968, c.282 (C.2A:168A-1 et seq.).

c. The State Treasurer shall update the information contained in the manual and the Department of the Treasury's Internet website periodically.

History

L. 1979, c. 460, § 8; amended 2014, c. 48, § 6, eff. Dec. 9, 2014; 2021, c. 179, § 11, effective October 20, 2021.

§ 52:7-18. Statement by notary public after change in name; filing; evidence of continuance of powers and privileges

a. If a notary public adopts a name different from that which the notary public used at the time the notary public was commissioned, before the notary public provides a signature to any record which the notary public is authorized or required to sign as notary public, the notary public shall make and sign a statement in writing and under oath, on a form prescribed and furnished by the State Treasurer, setting out the circumstances under which the notary public has adopted the new name. The statement shall state whether the new name has been adopted through marriage or civil union or by a change of name proceeding or otherwise, and such other information as the State Treasurer shall require.

b. The statement shall be filed in the office of the State Treasurer. Such statement, or a certified copy, shall be evidence of the right of the notary public to continue to exercise the powers and privileges and perform the duties of a notary public in the changed or new name.

History

L. 1979, c. 460, § 9; amended 2014, c. 48, § 7, eff. Dec. 9, 2014; 2021, c. 179, § 12, effective October 20, 2021.

§ 52:7-19. Certificate of notarial act

a. A notarial act shall be evidenced by a certificate. The certificate shall:

(1) be executed contemporaneously with the performance of the notarial act;

(2) be signed and dated by the notarial officer;

(3) identify the jurisdiction in which the notarial act is performed;

(4) contain the title of office of the notarial officer; and

(5) if the notarial officer is a notary public, indicate the date of expiration of the officer's commission.

b. A certificate of a notarial act is sufficient if it meets the requirements of subsection

a. of this section and:

(1) is in a short form set forth in section 21 of P.L.2021, c.179 (C.52:7-10.12);

(2) is in a form otherwise permitted by the law of this State;

(3) is in a form permitted by the law applicable in the jurisdiction in which the notarial act was performed; or

(4) sets forth the actions of the notarial officer which shall meet the requirements provided in P.L.1979, c.460 (C.52:7-10 et seq.), as amended and supplemented by P.L.2021, c.179 (C.52:7-10.1 et al.) and any other applicable laws of this State.

c. By executing a certificate of a notarial act, a notarial officer certifies that the officer has made the determinations specified by P.L.1979, c.460 (C.52:7-10 et seq.), as amended and supplemented by P.L.2021, c.179 (C.52:7-10.1 et al.).

d. A notarial officer may not affix the officer's signature to, or logically associate it with, a certificate until the notarial act has been performed.

e. If a notarial act is performed regarding a tangible record, a certificate shall be part of, or attached to, the record.

f. If a notarial act is performed regarding an electronic record, the certificate shall be affixed to, or logically associated with, the electronic record.

g. If the State Treasurer has established standards pursuant to P.L.1979, c.460 (C.52:7-10 et seq.), as amended and supplemented by P.L.2021, c.179 (C.52:7-10.1 et al.) for attaching, affixing, or logically associating the certificate, the process shall conform to the standards.

History

L. 1979, c. 460, § 10; amended 2014, c. 48, § 8, eff. Dec. 9, 2014; 2021, c. 179, § 13, effective October 20, 2021.

§ 52:7-20. Offenses resulting in non-appointment, no reappointment of notary public [Repealed effective October 20, 2021]

History

L. 1981, c. 487, § 1, eff. Jan. 12, 1982; amended 2011, c. 209, § 5, eff. Jan. 17, 2012; repealed by 2021, c. 179, § 37, effective October 20, 2021.

§ 52:7-21. Conviction for certain offenses, crimes; denial of appointment. [Repealed effective October 20, 2021]

History

L. 1981, c. 487, § 2, eff. Jan. 12, 1982; amended 2014, c. 48, § 9, eff. Dec. 9, 2014; Repealed by L. 2021, c. 179, § 37, effective October 20, 2021.

§§ 52:7-1 to 52:7-9. Repealed by L. 1979, c. 460, § 11, eff. Feb. 27, 1980.

NEW JERSEY ADMINISTRATIVE CODE
TITLE 17. TREASURY -- GENERAL
CHAPTER 50. NOTARY PUBLIC RULES
(EFFECTIVE UNTIL JANUARY 11, 2029)
SUBCHAPTER 1. GENERAL PROVISIONS

17:50-1.1 Purpose

(a) Adopted by the State Treasurer, and administered by the New Jersey Department of the Treasury, Division of Revenue and Enterprise Services, this chapter implements the provisions at P.L. 2021, c. 179.

(b) The rules streamline the commissioning process; clarify and expand upon the requirements to perform notarial acts; provide for the use of new technologies for notarization; and enhance the transparency and accountability of the office of notary public (office).

(c) In implementing the improvements in this chapter, the Department of the Treasury intends to: foster improved notarial service levels Statewide; place New Jersey on a strong footing in the notarial practice space nationally; and bolster the reliability and integrity of notarial practices in general. The ultimate beneficiaries of these

advancements will be New Jersey citizens and the State's business and legal communities that rely on notarial services.

17:50-1.2 Definitions

The following words and terms, when used in this chapter, shall have the following meanings, unless the context clearly indicates otherwise.

"Acknowledgment" means a declaration by an individual before a notarial officer that the individual has signed a record for the purpose stated in the record and, if the record is signed in a representative capacity, that the individual signed the record with proper authority and signed it as the act of the individual or entity identified in the record.

"Electronic" means relating to technology having electrical, digital, magnetic, wireless, optical, electromagnetic, or similar capabilities.

"Electronic signature" means an electronic symbol, sound, or process attached to, or logically associated with, a record and executed or adopted by an individual with the intent to sign the record.

"In a representative capacity" means acting as:

1. An authorized officer, agent, partner, trustee, or other representative for a person other than an individual;

2. A public officer, personal representative, guardian, or other representative, in the capacity stated in a record;

3. An agent or attorney-in-fact for a principal; or

4. An authorized representative of another in any other capacity. "Non-attorney applicant" means an applicant for an initial or renewal commission as a notary public who is not also a licensed attorney-at-law in this State.

"Notarial act" means an act, whether performed with respect to a tangible or electronic record, that a notarial officer may perform under the laws of New Jersey. The term includes:

1. Taking an acknowledgement;

2. Administering an oath or affirmation;

3. Taking a verification on oath or affirmation;

4. Witnessing or attesting a signature;

5. Certifying or attesting a copy or deposition; and

6. Noting a protest of a negotiable instrument.

"Notarial journal" means a compendium of each notarial act performed by a notary public and should include the:

1. Date and time of the notarial act;

2. Type of notarization;

3. Date of document notarized;

4. Type of document;

5. Identification provided as proof of identity;

6. Document signer's printed name;

7. Document signer's address;

8. Document signer's signature; and

9. Any other relevant information related to the notarial act.

"Notarial officer" means a notary public or other individual authorized by law to perform a notarial act.

"Notary public" means an individual commissioned by the State Treasurer to perform a notarial act.

"Official stamp" means a physical image affixed to or embossed on a tangible record or an electronic image attached to, or logically associated with, an electronic record.

"Person" has the meaning ascribed to it at N.J.S.A. 1:1-2.

"Record" means information that is inscribed on a tangible medium or that is stored in an electronic or other medium and is retrievable in perceivable form.

"Sign" means, with present intent to authenticate or adopt a record to:

1. Execute or adopt a tangible symbol; or

2. Attach to, or logically associate with, the record an electronic symbol, sound, or process.

"Signature" means a tangible symbol or an electronic signature that evidences the signing of a record.

"Stamping device" means:

1. A physical device capable of affixing to, or embossing, on a tangible record an official stamp; or

2. An electronic device or process capable of attaching to, or logically associating with, an electronic record an official stamp.

"Verification on oath or affirmation" means a declaration, made by an individual on oath or affirmation before a notarial officer, that a statement in a record is true.

17:50-1.3 Qualifications for office, scope of authority, and prohibited acts

(a) A person commissioned as a notary public in this State shall, at the time of appointment:

1. Be at least 18 years of age;

2. Be a legal resident of this State or have a place of employment or practice in this State; and

3. Not be disqualified to receive a commission pursuant to N.J.A.C. 17:50-1.5.

(b) A notary public who has been duly commissioned and qualified is authorized to perform the duties of a notary public throughout the State.

(c) A notary public may not perform a notarial act with respect to a record to which the notary public or the notary public's spouse or civil union partner is a party, or in which either of them has a direct beneficial interest. A notarial act performed in violation of this subsection is voidable.

(d) A notary public who is not licensed as an attorney-at-law shall not use or advertise the title of lawyer or attorney-at-law, or equivalent terms, in any other language, which means or implies that the notary public is licensed as an attorney-at-law in the State of New Jersey or in any other jurisdiction of the United States.

(e) Notaries public who advertise their services in any language are required to provide with such advertisement a notice that contains the following statement or translation of the following statement if the advertisement is not in English: "I am not an attorney licensed to practice law and may not give legal advice about immigration or any other legal matter or accept fees for legal advice."

17:50-1.4 Application procedures

(a) An applicant for commission as a notary public shall make application to the State Treasurer on a form prescribed by the State Treasurer. The application shall be endorsed by a member of the Legislature. Renewals shall be made in the same manner as the original application. All applications shall be submitted electronically through a means provided by the State Treasurer at www.nj.gov/njbgs.

(b) The fee for each application for a commission is $ 25.00 and is non-refundable.

(c) Within three months of the receipt of a commission, each notary public shall take and subscribe an oath to faithfully and honestly discharge the duties of the office and to make and keep a true record of all such matters as are required by law. The oath shall be sworn before the clerk of the county in which the notary public resides and shall be filed with said clerk.

(d) The oath of office of a non-resident notary public shall be taken and subscribed before the clerk of the county in which the nonresident notary public maintains the notary public's office or the county in which the nonresident notary public is an employee of a business with its domicile or primary place of business in this State. The oath shall be sworn before the clerk of the county in which the notary public resides and shall be filed with said clerk.

(e) Upon the administration of the oath, the clerk shall cause the notary public to endorse the certificate of commission and qualification and shall transmit the certificate to the State Treasurer within 10 days of the administration of the oath, through an electronic method provided by the State Treasurer.

(f) After the administration of the oath, the clerk shall provide a notice to the person that a notary public who is not licensed as an attorney-at-law shall not use or advertise the title of lawyer or attorney-at-law, or equivalent terms, in any language, which mean or imply that the notary public is, licensed as an attorney-at-law in the State of New Jersey or in any other jurisdiction of the United States. The notice shall also state that a notary public who advertises the notary public's services in any language, is required to provide with such advertisement a notice in the language of the advertisement, which contains the following statement or translation of the following statement if the advertisement is not in English:

> "I am not an attorney licensed to practice law and may not give legal advice about immigration or any other legal matter or accept fees for legal advice."

(g) The State Treasurer shall cancel and revoke the appointment of any notary public who fails to take and subscribe the oath within three months of the receipt of the commission and any appointment so canceled and revoked shall be null, void, and of no effect.

17:50-1.5 Commissioning of nonresidents; additional requirements

(a) A person who is not a legal resident of the State of New Jersey, but who maintains, or is regularly employed in, an office in this State or is an employee of a business with its domicile or primary place of business in this State and performs his or her employment duties remotely from a home office or a co-working space may apply for a commission by complying with the requirements at N.J.A.C. 17:50-1.4 and certifying the following additional information through the online commissioning site at www.nj.gov/njbgs:

1. The residence and the address of the applicant, and the office or place of employment of the applicant in this State; and

2. Once commissioned, any such nonresident notary public shall file online with the State Treasurer at www.nj.gov/njbgs a certificate showing any change of residence or change of the office or place of employment of the notary public in this State.

17:50-1.6 Name change; filing evidence of continuance of powers and privileges

(a) If a notary public adopts a name different from that which the notary public used at the time the notary public was commissioned, before the notary public provides a signature to any record that the notary public is authorized or required to sign as a notary public, the notary public shall make, sign, and file a statement in writing and under oath, on a form prescribed and furnished online at www.nj.gov/njbgs by the State Treasurer, setting forth the circumstances under which the notary public has adopted the new name.

(b) The statement shall state whether the new name has been adopted through marriage or civil union or by a change of name proceeding or otherwise, and such other information as the State Treasurer shall require. Such statement, or a certified copy, shall be evidence of the right of the notary public to continue to exercise the powers and privileges and perform the duties of a notary public in the changed or new name.

17:50-1.7 Denial, revocation, suspension, or limitation

(a) The State Treasurer may refuse to renew a commission of a notary public; or suspend, revoke, or otherwise limit the commission of a notary public for any act or omission that demonstrates that the individual lacks the honesty, integrity, competence, or reliability necessary to act as a notary public, including:

1. Failure to comply with P.L. 2021, c. 179 (N.J.S.A. 52:7-10 et seq.);

2. A fraudulent, dishonest, or deceitful misstatement or omission in the application for commission as a notary public submitted to the State Treasurer;

3. A finding against, or admission of liability by, the applicant or notary public in any legal proceeding or disciplinary action based on fraud, dishonesty, or deceit, including, but not limited to, a violation of section 1 at P.L. 1997, c. 1 (N.J.S.A. 2C:21-31) or section 1 at P.L. 1994, c. 47 (N.J.S.A. 2C:21-22), but nothing in this paragraph shall be deemed to supersede P.L. 1968, c. 282 (N.J.S.A. 2A:168A-1 et seq.);

4. A conviction of a crime of the second degree or above, but nothing in this paragraph shall be deemed to supersede P.L. 1968, c. 282 (N.J.S.A. 2A:168A-1 et seq.);

5. Failure by the notary public to discharge any duty required by any law, including P.L. 2021, c. 179 (N.J.S.A. 52:7-10 et seq.), any rules promulgated thereunder by the State Treasurer, and any other State or Federal law;

6. Use of false or misleading advertising or representation by the notary public representing that the notary is commissioned, licensed, or authorized to practice

or engage in work that the notary is not commissioned, licensed, or authorized to engage in;

7. In the case of a notary public who is not an attorney licensed to practice law, any of the following:

i. Giving legal advice;

ii. Acting as an immigration consultant or an expert on immigration matters;

iii. Otherwise performing the duties of an attorney licensed to practice law in New Jersey;

iv. A disciplinary or other administrative action resulting in a finding of culpability if the applicant holds any professional license regulated by the State; or

v. Creating or reinforcing, by any means, a false impression that the person is licensed to engage in the practice of law in this State or any other state, including, but not limited to, committing a violation of P.L. 1994, c. 47 (N.J.S.A. 2C:21-22) or P.L. 1997, c. 1 (N.J.S.A. 2C:21-31);

8. Failure to take and subscribe to the oath pursuant to section 8 of P.L. 2021, c. 179 (N.J.S.A. 52:7-14.) within three months of the receipt of a notary public commission;

9. Withholding access to, or possession of, an original record or photocopy provided by a person who seeks performance of a notarial act by the notary public, except where allowed by law; or

10. The denial of an application for notary public in another state; the refusal to renew in another state; or the suspension, revocation, or other limitation of the commission of the notary public in another state.

(b) When the State Treasurer denies an application for a notary public; refuses to renew a commission of a notary public; or suspends, revokes, or otherwise limits the commission of a notary public, the State Treasurer shall provide written notice to the applicant or commission holder.

(c) The written notice at (b) above shall include:

1. The name, email address, and telephone number of a contact person at the Division of Revenue and Enterprise Services;

2. The specific details concerning the reasons for the denial; and

3. Notification that the person can submit a request for a hearing, in writing, to the Division's contact person.

(d) The request for a hearing must be received within 20 calendar days from the date the person received the notice of the denial and must include a detailed statement of the reasons that the person believes the State Treasurer's determination is improper, together with supporting documentation, if any. It should also include a statement as to whether the person is represented by legal counsel, and if so, the name, address, and telephone number of said counsel.

(e) Upon the Division's timely receipt of the items set forth at (d) above, it shall determine whether a contested case exists, and if it does, the Division shall transmit the matter to the Office of Administrative Law for a hearing as a contested case.

(f) If the person has either failed to file a timely appeal or has expressly waived the right to appeal, the decision shall become a final decision.

(g) All hearings pursuant to this section shall be conducted in accordance with the Administrative Procedure Act, N.J.S.A. 52:14B-1 et seq., and 52:14F-1 et seq., and the Uniform Administrative Procedure Rules, N.J.A.C. 1:1.

(h) Any appeal of the final agency decision shall be solely to the Appellate Division of the Superior Court within time limits allowed by New Jersey Court Rule 2:2-3. The final agency decision shall include notice to the appellant of the right to file an appeal to the Appellate Division, the time frames, and related procedures.

17:50-1.8 Certificates and stamps

(a) All notarial acts shall be evidenced by a certificate and stamped by the notary public.

(b) Certificates shall:

1. Be executed contemporaneously with the performance of the notarial act;

2. Be signed and dated by the notarial officer;

3. Identify the jurisdiction in which the notarial act is performed;

4. Contain the title of office of the notary public; and

5. If the notarial officer is a notary public, indicate the date of expiration of the officer's commission.

(c) A certificate of a notarial act is sufficient if it meets the requirements at (a) above and:

1. Is in a short form as set forth at N.J.A.C. 17:50-1.10;

2. Is in a form otherwise permitted by the law of this State; and

3. Is in a form permitted by the law applicable in the jurisdiction in which the notarial act was performed.

(d) A notarial officer may not affix the officer's signature to, or logically associate it with, a certificate until the notarial act has been performed.

(e) If a notarial act regarding a tangible record is performed, a certificate shall be part of, or attached to, the record.

(f) If a notarial act regarding an electronic record is performed, the certificate shall be affixed to, or logically associated with, the electronic record.

(g) The official stamp of a notary public shall:

1. Include the name of the notary public, the title "Notary Public, State of New Jersey," and the notary public's commission expiration date; and

2. Be capable of being copied together with the record to which it is affixed or attached or with which it is logically associated.

(h) If a notarial act regarding a tangible record is performed by a notary public, an official stamp shall be affixed to or embossed on the certificate near the signature of the notary public to be clear and readable.

(i) If a notarial act regarding an electronic record is performed by a notary public and the certificate contains the information specified at (b) above, an official stamp must be attached to or logically associated with the certificate.

(j) Stamping device. A notary public is responsible for the security of the stamping device used by the notary public and may not allow another individual to use the device to perform a notarial act, except at the specific instruction of a notary public who cannot physically use the stamping device.

(k) The stamping device is the property of the notary public and not of the notary public's employer, even if the employer paid for the stamping device.

(l) If the stamping device used by the notary public is lost or stolen, the notary public or the notary public's personal representative shall notify the State Treasurer at https://www.nj.gov/treasury/revenue/revgencode.shtml of the loss or theft within 10 calendar days.

17:50-1.9 Requirement for individuals unable to sign

If an individual is physically unable to sign a record, the individual may direct an individual other than the notarial officer to sign the record with the individual's name. The notarial officer shall insert "Signature affixed by (name of other individual) at the direction of (name of individual)" or words of similar import.

17:50-1.10 Certificate forms

(a) The following short form certificates of notarial acts are sufficient for the purposes indicated if the requirements at N.J.A.C. 17:50-1.6 are satisfied.

1. For an acknowledgment in an individual capacity:

State of _____
County of _____

This record was acknowledged before me on _____ (date) by
_____
(Name(s) of individual(s))

_____
Signature of notarial officer
Stamp

_____
Title of office
My commission expires (date)

2. For an acknowledgment in a representative capacity:

State of _____
County of _____

This record was acknowledged before me on _____ (date) by
_____
(Name(s) of individual(s))

On _____(date)
As _____ (type of authority, such as officer or trustee) of (name of party on behalf of whom record was executed).

_____
Signature of notarial officer
Stamp

_____
Title of office
My commission expires (date)

3. For a verification on oath or affirmation:

State of _____

County of _____

Signed and sworn to (or affirmed) before me on _____ (date) by

_____

(Name(s) of individual(s) making statement)

_____

Signature of notarial officer
Stamp
Title of office
My commission expires (date)

4. For witnessing or attesting a signature:

State of _____

County of _____

Signed (or attested) before me on (date) _____

_____

(Name(s) of individual(s))

_____

Signature of notarial officer
Stamp
Title of office
My commission expires (date)

5. For certifying a copy of a record:

State of _____

County of _____

I certify that this is a true and correct copy of a record in the possession of
_____(name).

Dated _____ (date)

_____

Signature of notarial officer
Stamp

_____

Title of office
My commission expires (date)

17:50-1.11 Journal requirement

(a) A notary public shall maintain a journal of all notarial acts performed.

1. The journal may be created and maintained on a tangible medium or in an electronic format.

2. A notary public shall maintain only one journal at a time to chronicle all notarial acts, whether those notarial acts are performed regarding tangible or electronic records.

3. If the journal is maintained on a tangible medium, it shall be a permanent, bound register with consecutively numbered lines and consecutively numbered pages.

4. If the journal is maintained in an electronic format, it shall be in a permanent, tamper-evident electronic format.

(b) For each notarial act, the notary public shall record in the journal:

1. The date and time of the notarial act;

2. The type of notarial act, including, but not limited to, the taking of an acknowledgment, the taking of a proof of a deed, the administration of an oath, or the taking of an affidavit;

3. The name and address of each person for whom the notarial act is performed;

4. If the identity of the individual is based on personal knowledge, a statement to that effect;

5. If the identity of the individual is based on satisfactory evidence, a brief description of the method of identification and the identification credential presented, if any, including, if applicable, the type, date of issuance, and date of expiration of an identification document, or the name and signature of any identifying witness and, if applicable, the type, date of issuance, and date of expiration of a document identifying the witness; and

6. An itemized list of all fees charged for the notarial act.

(c) If a notary public's journal is lost or stolen, the notary public shall notify the State Treasurer within 10 days of the loss or theft at https://www.nj.gov/treasury/revenue/revgencode.shtml (select Notary application).

(d) The notary public shall:

1. Retain the journal for 10 years after the performance of the last notarial act chronicled in the journal; or

2. Write to the State Treasurer at https://www.nj.gov/treasury/revenue/revgencode.shtml for instructions on how to send or transmit the journal securely to the Division.

(e) On resignation from, or the revocation or suspension of, a notary public's commission, the notary public shall either:

1. Retain the journal for 10 years after the performance of the last notarial act chronicled in the journal; or

2. Write to the State Treasurer at https://www.nj.gov/treasury/revenue/revgencode.shtml for instructions on how to send or transmit the journal securely to the Division.

(f) On the death or adjudication of incompetency of a current or former notary public, the notary public's personal representative or guardian or any other person knowingly in possession of the journal shall, within 45 days, write to the State Treasurer at https://www.nj.gov/treasury/revenue/revgencode.shtml for instructions on how to send or transmit the journal securely.

(g) In lieu of maintaining a journal, a notary public who is an attorney-at-law admitted to practice in this State, who is employed by an attorney-at-law, or who is employed by, or acting as an agent for, a title insurance company licensed to do business in this State pursuant to P.L. 2001, c. 210 (N.J.S.A. 17:22A-26 et seq.), may maintain a record of notarial acts in the form of files regularly maintained for the attorney's law practice or the title insurance company's business activities, as the case may be.

17:50-1.12 Copy certification requirements

A notarial officer who certifies or attests to a copy of a record, or an item that was copied, shall determine that the copy is a full, true, and accurate transcription or reproduction of the record or item.

17:50-1.13 Forms of identification

(a) A notarial officer who takes an acknowledgment or verification of a record, or who witnesses or attests to a signature, shall determine, from personal knowledge or satisfactory evidence of the identity of the individual, that the individual appearing before the officer and making the acknowledgment has the identity claimed and that the signature on the record is the signature of the individual.

(b) Satisfactory forms of identification are as follows:

1. Personal knowledge. A notarial officer has personal knowledge of the identity of an individual appearing before the notarial officer if the individual is personally known to the notarial officer through dealings sufficient to provide reasonable certainty that the individual has the identity claimed.

2. Documentation. A notarial officer has satisfactory evidence of the identity of an individual appearing before the notarial officer if the notarial officer can identify the individual by means of:

i. A passport, driver's license, or government-issued non-driver identification card, which is current or expired not more than three years before the performance of the notarial act;

ii. Another form of government-issued identification, which is current or expired not more than three years before the performance of the notarial act, and which:

(1) Contains the individual's signature or a photograph of the individual's face; and

(2) Is satisfactory to the notarial officer; or

iii. A verification of oath or affirmation of a credible witness personally appearing before the notarial officer or using communication technology to appear before the notarial officer and personally known to the notarial officer or whom the notarial officer can identify based on a passport, driver's license, or government-issued non-driver identification card, which is current or expired not more than three years before the performance of the notarial act.

(c) A notarial officer may require an individual to provide additional information or identification credentials necessary to assure the notarial officer of the identity of the individual.

17:50-1.14 Requirements for use of communications technology

(a) If a notarial act relates to a statement made in, or a signature executed on, a record, the individual making the statement or executing the signature shall appear personally before the notarial officer or shall use communication technology to appear before the notarial officer.

(b) This section does not apply to a record to the extent it is governed by a law governing the creation and execution of wills or codicils, except as to a tangible record that is governed by a law governing the creation or execution of wills and codicils in which case, this section shall apply.

(c) As used in this section:

1. "Biometric identification" means using a human's physical or behavioral human features to digitally identify a person. Examples of biometric identification includes systems that use fingerprints and facial and voice patterns.

2. "Communication technology" means an electronic device or process that:

i. Allows a notarial officer and a remotely located individual to communicate with each other simultaneously by sight and sound; and

ii. When necessary and consistent with other applicable law, facilitates communication with a remotely located individual who has a vision, hearing, or speech impairment.

3. "Digital public key certificate" means an electronic credential issued by a trusted third-party that is used to identify a person who signed an electronic record.

4. "Dynamic knowledge-based authentication assessment" means identifying a person by asking the person a set of questions derived from public or private data sources for which the person has not been provided prior answers.

5. "Foreign state" means a jurisdiction other than the United States, a state, or a Federally recognized Indian tribe.

6. "Identity proofing" means a process or service by which a third person provides a notarial officer with a means to verify the identity of a remotely located individual by a review of personal information from public or private data sources.

7. "Outside the United States" means a location outside the geographic boundaries of the United States, Puerto Rico, the United States Virgin Islands, and any territory, insular possession, or other location subject to the jurisdiction of the United States.

8. "Remotely located individual" means an individual who is not in the physical presence of a notarial officer performing a notarial act.

(d) Before a notary public performs the notary public's initial notarial act pursuant to this section, the notary public must notify the State Treasurer electronically at www.nj.gov/njbgs that the notary public will be performing such notarial acts and identify the technologies the notary public intends to use.

(e) A remotely located individual may comply with this subchapter and N.J.S.A. 46:14-2.1.a and b (officers authorized to take acknowledgements and proofs) by using communication technology to appear before a notarial officer.

(f) A notarial act performed using communication technology for a remotely located individual is deemed performed in New Jersey and is governed by New Jersey law.

(g) A notarial officer located in this State may perform a notarial act using a communication technology for a remotely located individual, regardless of whether the individual is physically located in this State, if the notarial officer:

1. Ensures the remote session is interactive and secure, meaning the notary and person are viewing each other directly in real time and that the session cannot be viewed and/or recorded by an unauthorized party. The notarial officer must follow the security procedures of the National Notary Association, as supplemented (https://www.nass.org/sites/default/files/resolutions/2018-02/nass-support-revisedenotarization-standards-winter18_0.pdf);

2. Is able reasonably to confirm that a record before the notarial officer is the same record in which the remotely located individual made a statement or on which the remotely located individual executed a signature;

3. Obtains satisfactory identification for the remotely located individual that, for purposes of this subsection, means:

i. Visually verifies a proof of identity document as set forth at N.J.A.C. 17:50-1.13(b)2; and

ii. Uses personal knowledge to authenticate the individual's identity, or one of the following methods of identity proofing to authenticate the individual's identity, which are incorporated herein by reference, as amended and supplemented:

(1) Dynamic knowledge-based authentication that is provided online by a third-party and that substantially follows recommended practices for this form of identification, as set forth by any of the three following authorities: National Notary Association (January 2017), available at: https://www.nationalnotary.org/file%20library/nna/referencelibrary/model-enotarization-act.pdf; the National Association of Secretaries of State (February 19, 2018) at: https://www.nass.org/sites/default/files/resolutions/2018-02/nasssupport-revised-enotarization-standards-winter18_0.pdf; and the Mortgage Industry Standards Maintenance Organization (MISMO Remote Online Notarization Standards, Final Candidate Recommendation (CR) Version, Version 1. (2019). The Mortgage Industry Standards Maintenance Organization. Washington, D.C.) available at: www.mismo.org/standards-and-resources/emortgage-specifications/remot-onlinenotarization-standards;

(2) Biometric identity verification that is in substantial compliance with National Institute of Standards and Technology requirements, as set forth at Special Publication 800-76-2, https://nvlpubs.nist.gov/nistpubs/SpecialPublications/NIST.SP.800-76-2.pdf; and

(3) Digital public key certificate issued by a trusted third-party in substantial compliance with the National Notary Association's recommended practice, set forth at: https://www.nationalnotary.org/file%20library/nna/reference-library/model-enotarizationact.pdf, (Appendix II/Rule2, Public Key Certificate); and

iii. For a remotely located individual who is located outside the United States, ensures the record:

(1) Is to be filed with, or relates to, a matter before a public official or court, governmental entity, or other entity subject to the jurisdiction of the United States; or

(2) Involves property located in the territorial jurisdiction of the United States or involves a transaction substantially connected with the United States; and

iv. For the purposes of (g)3iii above, the act of making the statement or signing the record is not prohibited by the foreign state in which the remotely located individual is located;

4. Completes a certificate and stamp in accordance with the requirements set forth at N.J.A.C. 17:50-1.8(b), (c), (d), (e), (g), and (h); and

5. Creates an audio-visual recording of the performance of the notarial act.

(h) A notarial officer in this State may use communication technology to take an acknowledgement of a signature on a tangible record that is in the possession of the notary public if the record is displayed to, and identified by, the remotely located individual during the audio-visual session.

(i) A notarial officer may perform a notarial act with respect to a tangible record not physically present before the notarial officer, if:

1. The remotely located individual, during the audio-visual session:

i. Signs the record; and

ii. Signs a declaration, substantially in the following form, which is part of or securely attached to the record:

"I declare under penalty of perjury that the record to which this declaration is attached is the same record on which [name of notarial officer] performed a notarial act and before whom I appeared by means of communication technology on [date].

[Printed name of remotely located individual]
[Signature of remotely located individual"]; and

iii. Sends the record and declaration to the notarial officer not later than three days after the notarial act was performed; and

2. The notarial officer:

i. In the audio-visual recording required records the individual signing the record and declaration; and

ii. After receipt of the record and declaration from the individual, executes the notarial certificate and stamps the same as required at (g) above, which must include the following statement or words of similar import:

"I [name of notarial officer] witnessed, by means of communication technology, [name of remotely located individual] sign the attached record and declaration on [date]".

(j) A notarial act performed in compliance with (g) above is effective as of the date on which the declaration was signed by the remotely located individual.

(k) A notarial officer in this State may administer an oath to a remotely located individual using communication technology. The notarial officer shall identify the remotely located individual by obtaining satisfactory forms of identification pursuant to

(g) above, creating an audio-visual recording of the individual taking the oath, and preserving a copy of the audio-visual recording for 10 years.

(l) If a notarial act is performed pursuant to this section, the certificate of notarial act as required at (g) above or the certificate required at N.J.S.A. 46:14-2.1.c must indicate that the notarial act was performed using communication technology.

(m) A notarial officer, a guardian, conservator, or agent of a notarial officer, or a personal representative of a deceased notarial officer shall retain the audio-visual recording created pursuant to this section or cause the recording to be retained by a repository designated by or on behalf of the person required to retain the recording, for a period of 10 years.

17:50-1.15 Electronic notarization–general provisions and definitions

(a) A notarial officer may select one or more tamper-evident technologies to perform notarial acts with respect to electronic records. A person may not require a notarial officer to perform a notarial act with respect to an electronic record with a technology that the notarial officer has not selected.

(b) As used in this section:

1. "Tamper-evident" means that any change to a record shall provide evidence of the change.

2. "Logically associated with" means connecting, cross-referencing, or otherwise linking a certificate with a notarized record accurately and reliably, in a tamper-evident manner.

17:50-1.16 Requirements for electronic notarization

(a) With the exception of wills, codicils, and testamentary trusts, a notarial officer located in this State may perform a notarial act using a tamper-evident technology if the individual requesting the act appears in person before the notarial officer at the time of the act and the officer:

1. Obtains a satisfactory form of identification for the individual pursuant to N.J.A.C. 17:50-1.13; and

2. After executing the notarial act, completes an electronic certificate with an electronic signature and stamp, including all elements required at N.J.A.C. 17:50-1.13, and attaches the certificate and stamp to, or logically associates the certificate and stamp with, the notarized record.

(b) Before a notary public performs the notary public's initial notarial act with respect to an electronic record, the notary public shall notify the State Treasurer electronically at www.nj.gov/njbgs that the notary public will be performing notarial acts with respect to electronic records and identify the technology that the notary public intends to use.

(c) The notarial officer shall ensure that the officer's electronic signature stamp is reliable. To be considered reliable, an electronic signature and stamp must be:

1. Unique to the notarial officer;

2. Capable of independent verification;

3. Retained under the notary public's sole control; and

4. Attached to, or logically associated with, the electronic document in a tamper evident manner.

(d) The notary public shall not disclose any access information used to affix the electronic notary's signature and seal, except when requested by law enforcement, the courts, and with reasonable precautions, electronic document preparation, and transmission vendors.

17:50-1.17 Criteria for refusal to perform a notarial act

(a) A notarial officer may refuse to perform a notarial act if the officer is not satisfied that:

1. The individual executing the record is competent or has the capacity to execute the record;

2. The individual's signature is knowingly and voluntarily made;

3. The individual's signature on the record or statement substantially conforms to the signature on a form of identification used to determine the identity of the individual; or

4. The physical appearance of the individual signing the record or statement substantially conforms to the photograph on a form of identification used to determine the identity of the individual.

(b) A notarial officer may refuse to perform a notarial act, unless the individual presenting the record provides the officer with proof that refusal is prohibited by a State of New Jersey law other than N.J.S.A. 52:7-10 et seq.

17:50-1.18 Fees for notarial services

(a) Notarial officers may collect the following fees for services rendered:

1. For administering oaths, taking affidavits, taking proofs of a deed, and taking acknowledgments, $ 2.50 per act.

2. For administering oaths, taking affidavits, taking proofs of a deed, and taking acknowledgments of the grantors in the transfer of real estate, regardless of the number of such services performed in a single transaction to transfer real estate, $ 15.00.

3. For administering oaths, taking affidavits, and taking acknowledgments of the mortgagors in the financing of real estate, regardless of the number of such services performed in a single transaction to finance real estate, $ 25.00.

SUBCHAPTER 1. CONTINUING EDUCATION AND EXAMINATION REQUIREMENTS

17:50-2.1 Purpose

Adopted by the State Treasurer and administered by the New Jersey Department of the Treasury, Division of Revenue and Enterprise Services, this subchapter implements the provisions at P.L. 2021, c. 179, with respect to the establishment of education and testing requirements for non-attorney applicants for new and renewed notary public commissions. In implementing this subchapter, the Department intends to: foster improved notarial service levels Statewide; place New Jersey on a strong footing in the notarial practice space nationally; and bolster the reliability and integrity of notarial practices in general. The ultimate beneficiaries of these advancements will be New Jersey's citizens and the State's business and legal communities that rely on notarial services.

17:50-2.2 Education and testing requirements for initial notary public commissions

(a) A non-attorney applicant for an initial commission as a notary public shall complete a course of study that fosters the applicants' understanding of the statutes, rules, procedures, and ethical requirements documented in the State of New Jersey Notary Manual at www.nj.gov/njbgs. The State Treasurer shall ensure that the online course can be accessed through www.nj.gov/njbgs.

(b) Before being granted an initial notary public commission, a non-attorney applicant shall pass an online test at www.nj.gov/njbgs that confirms the applicant's understanding of the course content at (a) above. The State Treasurer shall ensure the online test and test instructions are accessible at www.nj.gov/njbgs and that the testing process is integrated with the State's online notary public commissioning system. The online system shall generate certificates of approval evidencing that applicants have passed the test. The system shall also record that applicants have passed the test and clear them to submit their notary public commission applications.

(c) The State Treasurer may charge up to $ 15.00 for administering each test.

17:50-2.3 Continuing education requirement for renewed notary public commissions

(a) A non-attorney applicant for renewal of a commission who has previously completed the educational and testing requirements at N.J.A.C. 17:50-2.2(a) and (b) at least one time, or who was commissioned for the first time before July 22, 2021, the effective date of P.L. 2021, c. 179, shall complete a continuing education course. The course shall focus on the statutes, rules, procedures, and ethical requirements documented in the State of New Jersey Notary Manual at www.nj.gov/njbgs. The State Treasurer shall ensure that the online course can be accessed at www.nj.gov/njbgs.

(b) The State Treasurer shall ensure the online course is integrated with the State's online notary public commissioning system. The online system shall provide certificates of approval evidencing that applicants have completed the continuing education course. The system shall also record that applicants have completed the course and clear them to submit their notary public commission applications. ■

About the NNA

Since 1957, the National Notary Association has been committed to serving and educating the nation's Notaries. During that time, the NNA° has become known as the most trusted source of information for and about Notaries and Notary laws, rules and best practices.

The NNA serves Notaries through its NationalNotary.org website, social media, publications, annual conferences, seminars, online training and the NNA° Hotline, which offers immediate answers to specific questions about notarization.

In addition, the NNA offers the highest quality professional supplies, including official seals and stamps, recordkeeping journals, Notary certificates and Notary bonds.

Though dedicated primarily to educating and assisting Notaries, the NNA supports implementing effective Notary laws and informing the public about the Notary's vital role in today's society.

To learn more about the National Notary Association, visit NationalNotary.org. ■

Index

Notes

Notes